Advance

Everyone is brilliant at something, and no one is brilliant at everything. Many are constantly told about all the things they don't have, can't do and are left feeling empty and excluded. *Migrant Magic* is the compelling antidote for all those who have been made to feel deficient, flawed and excluded. With Elham's deft and insightful touch, she is able to make many feel that they can, they should, and they will. Please give yourself the time to lean back, smile as you read and allow yourself to respond positively to this call for action. *Migrant Magic* will bring out the best in you.

Rene Carayol, MBE
Global Leadership Keynote Speaker,
Author, TV Commentator

Against the backdrop of social contestation and reactionary politics on the topic of immigration, Elham Fardad takes a different path. Her book is a narration of individual strength, but it is clear throughout that where migrants succeed, the winners are the societies, organizations, businesses and people they touch. Combining personal experience with that of countless other migrants in the UK, she brings warmth and humanity to stories that are contemporary but could transcend time and place to be a depiction of migration throughout modern history. This is a book of hope and validation, for migrants and for those that welcome them.

Sayeh Ghanbari
Partner, EY

Elham's *Migrant Magic* is a captivating journey into a world where the resilience of migrants transforms into extraordinary magic. Her writing, infused with heart and sincerity, is a beacon for young souls navigating exclusion. This insightful guide, born from genuine experience, provides practical tips for unlocking one's potential. Elham's profound understanding of the migrant experience creates a narrative that resonates deeply. As someone working with diverse talent and business leaders, I highly recommend *Migrant Magic*. It not only celebrates the triumphs of the marginalized but also serves as a testament to the limitless potential within us all.

Cynthia V. Davis, CBE
CEO and Founder, Diversifying Group

This is a book of inspiration and possibilities. It's a story that captures the essence of what it means to face impossible challenges and realize potential and ambition. Never have those experiences been truer than those who have had the word migrant attached to their life's journey. Elham has captured what lies at the very heart of this journey not only through her own experiences but also touching upon those of others who have gone through the same journey. In doing so, she covers the challenges, opportunities as well the values that migrants have contributed to both their own successes and that of the host country.

Nitin Parmar
Director, Developer Relations,
London Stock Exchange Group

Migrant Magic delves into the remarkable journeys of migrants who have harnessed their unique experiences as a source of strength. Throughout history, these individuals have transformed their perceived differences into a formidable power, propelling them to levels of success beyond their wildest dreams.

Within its pages, you will uncover a treasure trove of wisdom encapsulated in seven simple steps. These steps guide you in unlocking your own 'Migrant Magic', revealing your authentic abilities, distinct traits, and personal purpose. This new-found clarity will not only drive you forward but also grant you a sustainable competitive edge while upholding integrity.

This book is a must-read for several audiences. It speaks to those with immense potential, hindered only by their backgrounds, adversities, or disadvantages. It resonates with individuals from underrepresented backgrounds who find themselves in unfamiliar territories, yearning for relatable role models. Moreover, it extends its wisdom to organizational leaders, offering profound insights into nurturing a diverse talent pool with empathy and inclusivity.

Migrant Magic is a captivating journey filled with stories of remarkable mentors associated with Migrant Leaders, the charity founded by the author herself, Elham Fardad. Their stories will inspire, motivate, and ignite the spark within you.

I wholeheartedly encourage you to embark on this transformative journey and discover the magic that lies within you. *Migrant Magic* is more than just a book; it's a guide to realizing your fullest potential.

Chris Williams
Global Director – Diversity, Equity and Inclusion
CBRE Global Workplace Solutions

Really inspiring story of Elham and her dad! We can all relate, learn and get motivated. This book should infuse energy, passion and hope in life of all readers.

Harish Kumar
Managing Director, Alvarez & Marsal

Migrant Magic is a great book – a valuable coin with two sides. On one side, it is the migrant's story of hardship and success. On the other, it has some unique insights about the experiences of the diverse talent that are already part of organizations. *Migrant Magic* gives a viewing lens to leaders that they have never seen through before.

Rahul Welde
Former Executive Vice President, Digital
Transformation, Unilever

Elham's care and commitment towards the young and social mobility is exemplary. I know that *Migrant Magic* will be a much-needed companion to many young people. Elham's story is one that should be celebrated as a practical pathway for many of our country's youth. Young people have much to offer society and everything we can do as adults to be allies to them and open doors for them should be encouraged.

Saeed Atcha, MBE DL
Chief Executive Officer, Youth Leads

Right from the start, Elham's heartfelt reference to her father's story sets a powerful tone of resilience and triumph throughout the book. This inspiring theme is carried forward through her own captivating stories and those of many others, each sharing their unique perspectives on issues that resonate deeply with us all. I have no doubt that this exceptional book will make a profound difference in the lives of many. Kudos to Elham for her extraordinary work!

Daniyaal Anawar
Founder, GCSE Potential

Migrant Magic is a down-to-earth, heartfelt guide for anyone embarking on the journey of migration. Fardad's personal experiences, blended with real-life stories, offer both inspiration and practical advice. This book is more than just stories; it's a helping hand for those finding their way in new places. It's a relatable, honest look at the ups and downs of starting over, making it a must-read for anyone facing the challenges and opportunities of a new beginning.

Joe Seddon
Founder and CEO, Zero Gravity

migrant magic

magic

Transform your difference
into your superpower
for career success

ELHAM FARDAD

First published in Great Britain by Practical Inspiration Publishing, 2024

© Fardad, 2024

The moral rights of the author have been asserted

ISBN   9781788605632   (hardback)
       9781788605649   (paperback)
       9781788605656   (epub)
       9781788605663   (mobi)

Want to bulk-buy copies of this book for your team and colleagues? We can customize the content and co-brand *Migrant Magic* to suit your business's needs.

Please email info@practicalinspiration.com for more details.

**Practical Inspiration
Publishing**

I devote this book to a boy called Ali. He was born in a village in the county of Azerbaijan in Iran. A village with no water, no electricity and no school. As a ten-year-old he used to run many kilometres every day, in the harsh winters of Azerbaijan, to the next village so he could attend school. He had to run. There were frequent tales of wolves attacking children in winter. He loved school so much that he made sure he did his job on his father's farm so he would be allowed to go to school.

He was lucky enough for his academic gift to gain him a scholarship to study electrical engineering in the top technical university in Tehran. Fifty years on, the Academy of Sciences awarded him the highest accolade as the country's leading engineer for his services to building the cable industry.

That boy's name is Aligholi Fardad, he is my father and his story, humility and enduring integrity have inspired me all my life.

To my children Sara and Luis who are the joy of my life and who inspire me every day.

The author's profits from this book are being donated to charity.

Contents

Foreword
by Dr Yvonne
Thompson CBE DL

In the timeless swirl of migration, a narrative that is often shrouded in strife and struggle, germinates an unseen seed of unparalleled resilience, strength and unique prowess. As a migrant leader who has voyaged through the turbulent journey of relocation, adaptation and integration, I have found a resonant echo of my journey in Elham Fardad's *Migrant Magic*, feeling as though Migrant Magic has walked many miles in my shoes.

Immigrants, akin to myself and countless others, are more than mere ramblers; we are indeed the unwavering entrepreneurs, the unspoken leaders who bring a kaleidoscopic wealth of cultural diversity and knowledge, vivaciously enriching the landscapes of our adopted lands.

Elham has, with splendid mastery and empathetic intricacy, woven a tapestry that is palpably familiar, as I see something of myself in every chapter, yet remarkably enlightening to every migrant who has ventured into the perplexing domain of a new homeland. Her words don't just narrate; they cradle the 'migrant experience with a tenderness that can only emanate from a soul that has, herself, danced with the dichotomies of displacement and belonging. It is apparent that her steps have traversed the myriad pathways adorned with the multifaceted experiences of migration.

Migrant Magic is a sanctuary where the trials and tribulations of migration are acknowledged, yet it concurrently blossoms as a fertile ground where the seeds of leadership, with emotional intelligence and unmatched entrepreneurial spirit, are sown and nurtured. Elham embarks on a journey through seven judiciously curated chapters, exploring the realms of sacrifice, challenge, intuitive decision-making and ultimately, the undulating path to success, each stride delicately infusing the reader with the wisdom and strength that emanates through a lived lens.

This book serves as a luminary, shining light into the dark recesses of struggle that often encapsulate the migrant journey, revealing the latent, extraordinary powers that lie therein. Elham not only shares stories but she also unleashes a potent vault of practical advice and actionable steps, each chapter unfolding a new layer of understanding, each page a step towards unleashing the dormant magic within each migrant.

The narratives embedded within these pages transcend mere storytelling. They are a celebration, a validation and a sagacious guide that intertwines tales of triumph with practicable steps, progressively sculpting a pathway towards realizing an authentic, sustainable competitive advantage, deeply rooted in the fertile soils of integrity.

In a world that is progressively becoming a global village, yet paradoxically wrestling with the spectres of division and exclusion, *Migrant Magic* emerges not just as a book but as a movement, as a beacon of hope, leadership and an earnest call towards collective elevation and magnanimous societal give-back.

In essence, Elham Fardad does not merely hand us a guidebook but rather generously extends her hand, inviting us to join her on an enlightening journey towards unleashing our boundless, innate magic.

I'm proud to be a migrant and honoured to be invited to be part of this piece of UK history.

Migrant Magic is 'mi-story'.
Dr Yvonne Thompson CBE DL

What is this book about?

The world is changing rapidly and to succeed you have to adapt and take on challenging opportunities in new geographies, organizations and roles. But do you fear that feeling of being different, or do you embrace it and use it to your advantage?

Migrant Magic shows you how migrants have throughout history used their unique experiences to unleash a differentiation superpower to drive them to succeed beyond their own perceived abilities, resources and dreams.

Discover seven simple steps to unleash your own Migrant Magic: your unique authentic abilities, traits and personal purpose, to give you drive and sustainable competitive advantage with integrity.

Who is it for?

- Those striving to fulfil their potential but, despite their talent and hard work, their background, disadvantage and adversity are holding them back.

- People from under-represented backgrounds who have moved to a new environment and feel that they don't fit in and can't see relatable role models around them.
- Organizational leaders interested in developing their understanding of a diverse talent pool in order to gain deep empathy and inclusive ways to support and develop all colleagues.
- Anyone who would be inspired by hearing the stories of some of the most remarkable mentors at Migrant Leaders, the charity founded by the author, Elham Fardad.

Introduction

Every day the young give us a gift.

This book was not part of my life plan. But I guess plans sometimes change. Over the last five years since launching the charity Migrant Leaders, our mentees have given me the gift of their perspective every day. They have given me the privilege of making a difference to their life story. This book is my gift to them and to leaders who wish to understand what under-represented groups go through to succeed. Why they are the key to their organizations' success.

It was not easy but I had to dig deep into experiences that I had put in a box and locked up. I had to address some challenging topics such as racism, discrimination, integration, anger and fear in order to give my whole authentic self to this book and, importantly, to really benefit the reader.

On my journey to gain supporters for Migrant Leaders I heard many inspiring stories and realized how much we have in common with disparate groups who have gone through similar challenges. The key message here is look for what brings us together rather than what separates us. Our differences add spice to what unifies us.

We see many people working hard in life, frustrated that they are not getting the results or recognition they deserve. The beliefs you hold are fundamental to the effectiveness of your life decisions and efforts. In this book, I have aimed to help you achieve some paradigm shifts that will enable you to gain the success you deserve and the happiness we all wish for. This is fundamental not just for migrants but for all those who have experienced any form of injustice and inequality.

The other side of that coin is our duty to give back to the community, society and economy we are all part of. In so many situations, people attempt to first extract what is in it for themselves and then reluctantly execute their part of the bargain. I have shared in this book, how relationships and trust are the most valuable assets you will ever hold. To gain trust you need to truly care about the outcomes for others and to deliver on that first. Create so much value that you can afford to share the credit with others who deserve it.

They say it is never too late, and I do wholeheartedly believe you can turn around your life at any time. I certainly intend to keep learning throughout my life and to keep adding value for as long as my capabilities are useful. But getting the timing right makes the journey of life easier for you and the results more spectacular. As such I have explained in this book why and how you can find your purpose, recognize your talents and create momentum.

Why Migrant Magic?

People asked me why I called this book *Migrant Magic*. I said to them that there were a few times when Migrant Leaders supporters asked me how the charity had progressed so solidly and so fast, gaining the support of so many incredible people and organizations. My intuitive answer to them was Migrant Magic! The incredible drive, determination and capabilities that come with having lived with and risen above the challenges that us migrants have experienced.

In my quest to recruit Migrant Leaders mentors I have spoken to over a thousand corporate executives over the past five years, some of whom were migrants themselves. I have brought to you some of the rawest conversations and personal stories they shared. I have also shared in no particular order many of my own life anecdotes in order to illustrate my life lessons and experiences. I have written this book in a way so that you can read in any order the chapters that speak to you.

Before you start reading this book, know one thing. That you are special, really special. Keep an open heart and mind to really reflect on who you want to be. Know that you can achieve anything you set your mind to.

Chapter 1

Fulfil your potential to make sense of what you have sacrificed

Early on in my youth I had a run of obstacles one after the other. I now know that these were typical migrant family challenges, which for me included family breakup, visa and financial problems, and the responsibility of looking after family from a young age.

At 18, I was a young Iranian migrant growing up in Birmingham; I had nothing left, but I knew one thing. That I loved learning and wanted to succeed in life. I desperately wanted to go to university but I had a problem. Having moved to the UK only a few years before, I would be counted as a foreign student and couldn't possibly afford the fees even if I worked full-time. I had already saved money by teaching maths, working in shops and buying and selling perfumes door to door. But I decided to give that money to my mother for my little brother. Once again, I was penniless.

I decided that I had no choice but to somehow persuade the British government to count me as a home student. It is incredible how empowering it is to know what you want to achieve and that you actually have no options. You dig deep and find the one solution that there is and know that you must make it work.

I camped outside Birmingham city council offices for three days in a row until someone agreed to take me inside so I could explain. I was lucky. I was put in front of people who listened to me about wanting to go to university, getting a good job and paying my taxes. I shared with them what that would mean to me personally. A few weeks later, I received a letter that confirmed me as a home student. I was surprised by how that felt. The letter was doubtless a lifeline to my future and that felt great, but even greater was the feeling of being counted as one of them. To me the letter was also a confirmation of the Brummie that I had long felt I am. That was my first experience of what inclusion truly feels like and I vowed to serve this country my whole life.

I went to university and life wasn't plain sailing but I rose to the challenge and by the time I was 25, I had a degree and had qualified as a professional accountant with 'first time passes'. My big break came when I joined GE as a financial controller. I remember the first few weeks at GE was Six Sigma training, and I called my father and told him that I couldn't believe that they were actually paying me to do what I love.

There were also some dark moments when the anxieties that accompanied my experiences would come back. I asked myself many times, why me? Why did the challenges have to be so relentless? What more could I have achieved if the path had been smoother or at least closer to what seemed typical or an ordinary path for others? Would I have this anxiety for the rest of my life? So, in a moment of resentment if I am honest, I asked my father that question: why me? He answered with equal emotion with: why not you? He went on to say that you are lucky to be in a country full of opportunities and good people. In many countries, he said, millions are born in the streets and they die in the street. That could have been you. You are no better or worse than anyone else and if you want something you have to work for it. In that moment, I decided to use my potential not only for achievement but to help me process and make sense of everything that I and my family had lost and sacrificed by moving to a different country. Fulfilling my potential would help me make sense of what we had all sacrificed.

Happiness is the real success

People often attach conditions to happiness. They say I will be happy when I have accomplishments and wealth, when I am secure. I used to be one of them. I only allowed myself to be happy if I was productive and achieved success. As time went by, I began to notice a pattern. The periods of my life where I was the most productive, creative and successful were when I was already happy. The success followed the happiness, rather than the other way around.

I noticed that as I heard about injustice or inequities in society, I felt the urge to intervene. I wanted to have an impact on the world that goes beyond my individual success and wealth creation.

The field of positive psychology looks at what makes people thrive. This is where your personal perception of life really matters. I discovered that for me my whole life supports my vision. I realized that in order to be truly successful, I need harmony, happiness and security in my family life. Perhaps because it is something that I didn't always have when I was growing up.

> Success follows happiness rather than the other way around. In order to thrive, look for what has meaning to you.

I decided at an early age that I wanted to fulfil my career potential and be a brilliant mum one day. The formula I came up with was to go into fifth gear in the first 10 years of my career so that when I do have children, I can prioritize them and still use the career momentum that I had created.

There are many different ways of achieving the same objectives. Speaking to Nilofar Bhurawala, Solutions Architect at a multinational IT services and consulting company, she expressed that she doesn't see a family versus career trade-off and that different areas of your life complete each other. She explained:

I was married at the age of 18 and had my first child at 20 and second child at 24. I came to the UK as a dependant immigrant. My journey as a woman, migrant and without a first degree was full of obstacles, it still is. I eventually managed to get an MBA in 2019 from Royal Holloway and my work experience supported my application. The reason I would like to mentor the younger generation is to give an example of my journey that shows you can have both family and career. Now at the age of 37, I am a senior IT executive who has worked with large consulting firms and has a fulfilling life.

Once you have decided what your life strategy and approach is, how do you then deliver on that?

You must aim high for your aspirations, because nothing feels as bad as regret. Knowing that you didn't do everything you could have done. But it is not all on you. Social support is one of the biggest issues that migrant families face. Sometimes an individual may have family and community support as long as they fit in the expected cultural mould. Lee Chambers is a workplace wellbeing expert and he explains the twists and turns in his quest to reach high for a life in which he would have no regrets:

I've always been ambitious, but never really knew what I wanted to do. My parents wanted me to be the first in my family to go to university, and I made it there, but struggled with the pressure and lack of role models that looked and sounded like me. I ended up dropping out, but after working on myself for a year, I went back and managed to graduate. I then secured a graduate scheme in finance, and my parents were delighted. But I struggled in that environment at times, and was made redundant due to the economy.

His first challenge was finding a path that would lead to his own happiness:

But again, this challenging time inspired me to launch a business, and grow that successfully for the next five years. With no safety net and little support, it was a risk, but we often regret the things we didn't do. I learnt many lessons being a leader, but after losing the ability to walk due to illness, I learnt just how important having a support network around me was, as I couldn't do the simplest things for myself.

Through adversity he discovered more characteristics in himself and many supportive relationships along the way, which led to today:

It was a very difficult time for me, yet it was in this adversity that I stopped to realize how important having gratitude is, and how much my daughter being born drove me to learn to walk again. But it did something else, and it gave me the threads of purpose to build the business I have today, which works in the field of wellbeing, very different than my first business. The lesson from my journey, which I still feel at the start of, is to take opportunities that come your way, some may fail but every one will be a lesson. Build a support network, as you never know when you will need it, and a diverse network will expand your horizons. But most importantly, never underestimate the potential you have, as it will always be more than you know.

Sometimes the needs of migrant and other disadvantaged families are so acute that they may prioritize immediate physical needs. I asked Professor Joanna Clarke, a Consultant Chartered Psychologist, what in her view is the key to happiness, and she shared with me why social connection is actually essential:

The bottom line is that we need each other. Since the dawn of the human time, those in strong social groups thrived. And the same is still true today. Social connection boosts both physical and mental health, and loneliness can kill.

She described how this issue came to the surface in extreme circumstances during the Covid pandemic:

Being told to socially distance during the pandemic was like telling us to not drink water. The isolation and loneliness brought on by shutting ourselves away has caused untold harm. What we needed to do was physically distance (to stay physically safe) and socially connect (to stay psychologically safe). But even social connection through our array of sophisticated technologies is not enough in the long run.

She advises us to seek happiness through social connection and support:

We need to be in each other's presence because, as we're learning, our whole body and mind is impacted for the better when in the presence of those we love and care for. So, make special time to be with those who matter to you, who see you, who get you, and can respond to your needs as you can for them. It doesn't need to be a whole tribe, just a small group of your special people. And make sure to have your mind present as well as your body to get the full benefit of the social support they offer.

In my quest to recruit Migrant Leaders mentors I have spoken to well over a thousand senior executives across more than one hundred companies. It struck me that what they have in common isn't their gender, race or even background. It is how their diverse experiences have shaped their characters. It is their common search for happiness and the refusal to give up, despite the odds against them.

The Institute for Fiscal Studies (IFS) Deaton Review highlighted exactly what the odds are against migrant children despite their educational success. Migrant children in the UK have double the rate of university degrees compared to the white majority. Despite this, they are significantly behind in attaining professional jobs and managerial progression. For some groups this might feel insurmountable. Among second-generation Pakistani and Bangladeshi women 39–50% attained a university degree. But overall, the same group performed 9–12%

lower in attaining professional or managerial jobs than the white majority.

If you are looking for reasons to use the overall odds against you as justification to give up, I can share more statistics with you about under-representation and structural barriers in different professions. But that is not going to help you.

Additionally, there are internal pressures within families. Traditionally, parents advised their children to go into professions which would welcome them, for instance steering girls into so-called female-friendly professions. It is as though under-representation in certain professions is seen as reducing your odds of success.

I was lucky. Every time my community, and women in particular, implied that my education was only so that I marry well, my father whispered in my ear. He told me that as a girl I must fulfil my educational and professional potential even more, in order to pave the way in the future for my children. He knew this because he had seen the impact of extremely biased gender dynamics in his village.

For this reason, every time I speak with any executive who has beaten the odds, my heart goes out to them because I know what it took to achieve that. I feel humbled to speak to people like Risham Nadeem who is a Business Director in a global customer insights agency. She explained to me how she has pushed against the odds:

> I'm a first-generation Pakistani immigrant and the first in my family to go to university in this country. I read History at the University of Oxford and I am now a Business Director at a world leading innovation and insight consultancy that provides services to iconic brands. Prior to doing this, I freelanced and started my career at a leading global IT consultancy. Resilience and generosity are values that have shaped my approach to my life and career, and I can see clearly how my upbringing – and my parents' own struggle – contributed to this.

The classic happiness formula talks about the relationship between your expectations and your capabilities and resources. That holds true, but it is a very simple way of looking at happiness. I respect the original happiness formula but I think it could inadvertently feed the mentality that everyone has their place in society fixed at birth. I do not accept that and I want to live in a society where anything is possible for anyone.

There are ways to boost your resources, such as money, energy and health. There are ways to discover your capabilities by building your skills and networking. But I always thought the formula was missing a coefficient. An individual's ability to boost their resources and discover their capabilities is sometimes transformed through extreme experiences and hardship, revealing what I would call resource elasticity and capability agility. Qualities that migrants often discover when they are resilient in extreme conditions. They ignite the migrant happiness formula.

In other words, take a leap of faith with me and believe in yourself and your ability to discover what makes you happy. Don't fear the odds against you. If you beat the odds, that will one day be your differentiator. Something that distinguishes you from everyone else.

Pay your parents back with the migrant formula

When I launched the Migrant Leaders charity back in 2017, I just wanted to solve a problem for a group of people I cared about. I really thought this will be me bringing all the skills and contacts I had gained from the private sector to help communities. What I hadn't expected was how much I would learn, not just about the charity sector, but also about diverse people.

The most I have learnt is from the young mentees who explain their challenges, hopes and dreams. Before I knew it, they had in five years turned me back into the 16-year-old I used to be. Fearless, confident, full of energy.

One of my favourite activities is reading through their applications to our programme, and I found it interesting that well over half of them mention that their motivation in joining our programme is to succeed in life and buy their parents a house and pay them back for their hard work and sacrifice. The vast majority have parents who work hard in manual and low-paid jobs as factory workers, drivers, care workers, in order to provide their children a chance. They effectively tell their children that education is their lever for social mobility. I see many young people on our programme producing the very best academic results for this country. That is what I call the migrant formula, where the first generation sacrifices everything in the hope that education will open opportunities for the next generation.

Mariama Nadworna, Marketing Manager at a national building society, came to the UK as a young baby with her parents from Sierra Leone:

> My father had a Master's degree but both him and my mother ended up working in manual jobs as a cleaner and a petrol station attendant.

They accepted that humbly because they wanted us kids to succeed in the UK. This was even after my grandfather came from a village, educated himself, paid for his own university and became the education minister in Sierra Leone. We went back several steps in order to go forward in the UK.

No matter what social class or educational level they enter the host country with, this unwritten shared understanding seems to be adopted across migrant communities. People sometimes misunderstand and judge migrants of different backgrounds. The migrant formula unites all migrants, whatever their socioeconomic background or ethnicity. There are educated middle-class migrants who also go through this sacrifice and hardship.

The migrant formula means our parents sacrificed themselves for our success. To accept that with gratitude we have to turn that into power and find our happiness and success.

Others launch their own businesses, pharmacies, corner shops, and put everything they earn into the private education of their children because they want to give them something they didn't have and that they perceive as a valuable investment. I have discovered nuances about people's backgrounds a good few years after I considered them a friend. I remember Charlotte Harvey, Managing Director Corporate Affairs at a global PR agency, telling me:

> You may be surprised by how I grew up with my migrant mixed raced mother and that I only went to private school because I got a full merit-based scholarship.

I felt proud of her and proceeded to tell her that I went to three different state schools in three years. Despite the grades I got in 11 GCSEs just a couple of years after entering the UK, as recent migrants we didn't even know such scholarships existed for us to apply to. I often wonder how things might have been different, but I quickly remind myself of the characteristics I may not have discovered had I not gone through this journey. This is where they say it was destiny.

The other motivation I notice in the young mentees is that they are in a rush to succeed and help their families. I always tell them that you need to first succeed yourself in order to support your parents. You need to succeed on solid ground with a technical or sector focus, developing skills that use your natural talents. When I say that, I remember my friend Frank Omare, Senior Director at a leading multinational business software company, who with a quietly proud face described how his single mother brought them up:

> As the oldest of four there was always a pressure on me to lead the way. My mother came here in the 1960s, very hard working and she taught me everything about honesty, determination, hard work and integrity. We had nothing but I had everything I needed. She was a role model to me. She had two jobs, worked in a factory during the day and had a cleaning job at night but she created an air of determination to do our work. We never wanted to let my mother down. I am proud of my brothers and sister. I went on to study chemical engineering, subjects I was passionate about. My brother studied mechanical engineering. My other brother studied business and my sister is a solicitor. We flourished within a disciplined culture.

Frank and his siblings each carved out their own success path but they learnt from their family's best qualities. Characteristics that no amount of education, money or luck can train you in.

Speaking to so many executives of all backgrounds, I realized that sense of cultural and family heritage continues for many generations. Supporters of the charity have one thing in common, that they were outsiders who eventually succeeded. There are supporters who came from white British working-class families who were then the first generation to go to university. There was one supporter who explained to me why he would like to support Migrant Leaders and described his family's story, starting with his great-grandfather who was a Polish Jew who survived.

We are united with everyone in this country who ever felt like an outsider, who through the migrant formula and their family's success story, support their families and give back to society. You are part of this country and we are all with you throughout your journey.

Think of what you want to be known for

After I landed that financial controller job in GE at the age of 25, I spent the next 10 years as a finance director at GE and News Corp and another 10 years in EY working with some of the best client companies on their operational problems. At EY they often talked about deciding what you want to be famous for in order to be lined up for promotion. They were talking about technical and sector specialization and personal branding. In my case this seemed like a logical decision based on my deep experience of process improvement, analytics and cost reduction. But somehow that didn't feel enough for me. The jobs I really flourished in involved transformation, strategic growth in the markets that the client operates in and then operational turnaround to ensure that growth is profitable and sustainable. I knew what success is supposed to feel like.

It was through launching the Migrant Leaders charity that I discovered my purpose. The success of the charity was a reminder to me of how important your motivations are. The answer to what you should want to be known for is not in *what*, it is in *why*. Asad Maqsood, a barrister, explains why representation in the legal profession is his key motivation. His journey was full of uncertainty and hardship:

> I was a migrant from Pakistan in my late teens with no money or qualifications. I had no professional connections or guidance to draw upon. I chose the cheap but painful distance learning mode for the qualifying law degree and became the first generation to graduate. The way my unique route to the Bar facilitated and promoted my pro bono work, I cannot see that happening in a conventional route. Even before I became a barrister, there was hardly anyone around me who had not already benefited from my legal training. My struggle made me who I am, and when I say I

am 'self-made', that word has a whole different meaning for me than most. Break the barriers and discover that meaning.

Asad experienced every day how difficult this was for him and others like him. Through this he discovered what he wants to be known for, and his contribution to representation in the legal profession:

> Despite surmounting my obstacles and continuing as a successful practitioner, further career progression at the Bar for someone with my background has its own hurdles. No country is perfect, and although there is still a lot of work to be done towards diversity and inclusion here, I must say that I have huge respect for this country for the progress that has been made here thus far and I am proud that I contribute in some way to representation in the legal profession.

This representation in the legal profession matters. Similarly to other professions, legal professionals need to be representative of and have an understanding of the clients they represent. For the criminal justice system, for instance, this representation is vital. The proportion of staff and practitioners in the criminal justice system organizations from white ethnic groups ranges between 79% (Ministry of Justice) and 93% (Court Judges). There is an under-representation of minority ethnic groups among senior practitioners. At the same time, there is an over-representation of people of colour in prisons, with over half of under-17-year-olds and almost a third of adults in prison being from minority ethnic groups (MoJ Statistics on Race and The Criminal Justice System 2018). Migrant Leaders mentor, Professor Mary Bosworth, explains:

> There is a hierarchy within the criminal justice system and people are moving into roles but perhaps not always into the most senior roles or there would be clustering. This appears to impact how the justice system operates and that is why representation matters.

When it comes to building trust in the system, nothing speaks louder than the stories of young people with their hopes and dreams to contribute to society. Migrant Leaders mentee, Adrienne Larmond, expresses:

> My parents are from Jamaica. I can confidently say I am proud of the progress that my parents achieved immigrating to England, however, I felt that I did not know enough about the variety in career choices post-university. When I joined Migrant Leaders, they introduced

me to different mentors to make sure I find a mentor I feel connected to and trust. My mentor Zeynep from Migrant Leaders really encouraged me to aim high and reach for my dreams. This support and coaching together with the Migrant Leaders workshops and programme meant that I applied for Oxford feeling safe, and I got in!

History is full of successful people with what appear to be superhuman abilities. When it comes to migrants, some of them get through the seemingly impossible odds because something in their migrant journey motivated them to use that force behind their emotions for good. Those migrants who find and use their superpower go on to phenomenal success. In the UK almost a quarter of the highest-paid jobs are filled with migrants. Of the top 1% earning more than £128,000, 24% moved to the UK as adults. Migrants represent just 15% of the UK population.

Among successful migrants there will of course be a mixture of people. Those who came to the UK with skills, experience and resources. Others who came with nothing but their hopes and family values that drove them towards success. In both cases fame should not really be about you, but about the beneficiaries, customers, colleagues and the companies whose problems you want to solve.

Once you know your why, the how is easier to work out, because by then you have a vision for the end game, you understand what motivates you and your next task is to discover what you are really brilliant at. Not just good at, but brilliant at.

 Find what really motivates and drives you. Once you know your real why, the how is easier to work out.

One of our charity's patrons, Rene Carayol MBE, explains in his book *Spike* that there are no losers. Everyone has something they are great at, at least one inherent strength. He tells us that we also have to be honest with ourselves when developing and showcasing those strengths:

> It is equally important for ethnic minority talent to hold up a mirror to themselves as it is for organizations to support them.

The key for me is the congruence between what your natural talents are, and finding a market place that is desperate for those exact abilities. In other words where you can add the most measurable value. Add to that a customer problem or a beneficiary group you really care about, perhaps due to the hardships you have gone through, and you have begun to find your migrant magic.

Chapter 2

The obstacles are part of the journey and reveal your unique gifts

Having persuaded Birmingham city council to give me home student status, I went to university and immediately got a job working three nights a week in a restaurant. The restaurant was a few miles away and I used to cycle in the freezing wind in Hull on my 20-quid rattling bicycle to get there. I was happy to be earning the money I needed.

After six weeks working there, I was beginning to get suspicious. The restaurant owner kept making excuses every week as to why he couldn't pay me. He didn't have the cash in the safe, he had a cash flow issue that week, he paid the suppliers this week. After six weeks I decided to find another job but I couldn't just cut my losses, I needed the money. So, I cycled to his restaurant the next night when I didn't have a shift as I still didn't want to let him down on a night that he thought I had a shift. I told him that I was there to collect all the wages he owed me. He made the same excuses as usual. I said I would not go away until he paid me what he owed me. He threatened to call the police, and I told him if he didn't, I sure would, because it must be illegal not to pay people for their work. He reluctantly paid me and even asked would I come to work the next night. I respectfully declined and told him something about having standards.

They talk about the characteristics of having grit and determination but during that period in my life I was in survival mode. I didn't have time to pause and consider what I was going through as adversity, nor did it occur to me that this grit would one day serve me. But this and many other experiences ended up being much of what I am today.

At 25, I landed the GE financial controller job, and I remember the very supportive CEO told me, as I started the job, not to worry myself with the past due debt they hadn't been able to collect from a power station company in the Middle East. This was debt that this other company owed GE which as the new financial controller would be my responsibility to collect for GE. I thanked him for that support but asked him not to write the debt off and to give me a couple of months so I could try to collect some of the debt. I knew that a Middle Eastern power station was not going to respond well to a young Iranian female working in finance. So, I decided to say it like it is and declare my intentions. I called the client manager and explained that I was the new financial controller, that I was originally from Iran and this was a new job for me, that I was determined to do well at. I said that we clearly owed him an apology for not meeting their standards and that I would not give up until I had brought him all the missing documentation, components, signatures and anything else that he stipulated. I could tell the client manager was smiling on the phone when he told me that he had a daughter just like me and that he knew I was not going to leave this. The next few weeks were the most collaborative working experience I have had, where he and I talked every few days to put together everything needed, and my new GE colleagues within the management team were intrigued. They were beyond happy when I ended up collecting most of that very significant debt. During the first six months in the job, all sorts of new things were thrown at me and I was flying. It felt like a strange combination of fear and excitement every time I had a new challenge. They were very happy, so I thought about the equity of this carefully and I decided I was going to ask them for something that I had long dreamed of doing.

I practised in front of a mirror all weekend and then on the Monday sat down with my boss for the usual weekly review. He expressed how happy he was and I said how I enjoyed working with everyone there and how much more I planned to contribute in various areas of the business. I explained that something that would be immensely helpful to my role would be to have an MBA from the University of Warwick and that I had an offer to study for their Executive MBA in my own personal time but that I couldn't otherwise afford the university fees. I said it would be pretty tax efficient if GE paid for the MBA. He smiled and explained that even though GE didn't pay for MBAs, given their famed in-house training, he would try.

I am really glad he did and that GE agreed because what he didn't know is what I had done to get that offer from the University of Warwick. When I applied to their Executive MBA, they rejected me, quite rightly, citing insufficient length of experience. They offered me the full-time MBA but I really valued learning by working with the more experienced students on an executive programme and there was no way I was going to slow down the career momentum I had gathered. So, I called their admissions department and insisted on an appointment for an interview. I promised if they rejected me after the interview, I would gratefully accept that outcome. The interview was with a very senior academic course leader and 90 minutes into the interview I was enjoying the conversation so much that I couldn't believe it when he said, 'you realize you are going to be the youngest Warwick Executive MBA student ever'. Twenty years later, I am still devoted to Warwick and give lectures to their Master's students.

Don't regret your migrant journey

We sometimes regret how we played the cards we have been dealt in life. Regret is a word used in a negative context; we know how bitter regret feels because it is about a past we cannot change. Often regret results from our own decisions, actions or inaction. For this reason, I make many decisions by asking myself what is the outcome I would regret.

But we often use our fear of regret to avoid chasing our dreams. Ask yourself how many people you know who claim they had the idea for eBay or the many other global businesses and yet did nothing with their idea?

People think ideas are born perfect. I discovered by launching Migrant Leaders that often the best ideas are those that seem unrealistic to others but our gut tells us we are onto something. Ideas are not born perfect; they are developed through a rigorous process. I had a feeling for the idea for Migrant Leaders in my gut early in 2017 and then, given my EY client work and young family to look after, did nothing with it. But once again luck was on my side.

In the summer of 2017, we went on holiday to China. For possibly the first time in my life I was mysteriously hit with really heavy jet lag. We would go to bed in our family hotel room at around midnight, and then everyday like clockwork I would wake up at 4 am wide awake. The first night I kept quiet, looking at the hotel room ceiling in the dark, not wanting to wake up my family. It then occurred to me maybe I could use this to my advantage and write up that charity development programme I had in my mind. I ended up in our hotel bathroom doing the high-level design of the programme over two weeks in China every day from 4 am to 9 am while my family were asleep. By the end of the holiday, I realized I had a decent programme and plan but I did question whether it was a bit too much or ridiculous. So, I decided to test it with friends and trusted ex-colleagues and, importantly, with young people through a youth conference. I also set up meetings with people I knew in the community for when we landed in London. I knew that I must be brave with my 'ridiculous' idea but take it through a robust consultation process. I really thought they would congratulate me on how leading practice the programme design was, because I tried to combine my personal and professional experience with the leadership programmes I had been on at GE and EY.

I listened to much feedback and the most useful came from a 16-year-old girl who got quite emotional when she told me this was not how young people learnt these days. I was taken aback but I took a breath and asked her to tell me more. She explained that all the training, connections and mentoring were good but it was too rigid by telling them they must do one module per month, and in the order they are told to. It is as a result of that conversation and continuous improvement that the Migrant Leaders programme is now so dynamic, flexible and modular in its delivery.

Often our dreams seem far away, but having the discipline to keep going, and not regretting the hardship you experience as a migrant, does eventually lead to success. Hicham Daoud, Business Analysis Consultant, at a FTSE 250 IT training company, explains:

> I came to the UK as a refugee and after 24 years, in July 2022 I finally got my indefinite leave to remain. If I had decided to regret that tough journey, I would have cheated myself out of the engineering degree I completed at the University of Leeds. I am now studying for a Master's in global finance analytics at King's College, while working full-time.

One of the challenges migrants face is that having experienced adversity and failure, they fear regret. Talking to Purnima Sen, Chief People and Compliance Officer at a technology training company, reminded me why you must take responsibility and welcome your failures as well as your successes:

> Having started my own ice business in India at the age of 21, it was a big step to sell it and come to the UK for my MBA. Having won a scholarship to do so, I arrived here alone and scared but full of hope. I was in 1994 a single

brown woman, full of anticipation and the plan was to do everything thrown at me with honesty and commitment. Through hard work, diligence, persistence and work ethic, I built, not just a life, but made many friends and allies. Now with three beautiful girls (and a dog!), and a thriving career I feel it has all paid off.

Consider what success characteristics your purpose and plan need, what limited you in the past, and how you can develop and gain support to challenge yourself and maintain the courage not to let those same characteristics limit you. Equally, notice what worked well for you in your previous phenomenal successes. As a migrant you go through more extreme experiences and conditions than the so-called average person. This diversity of experience would have led to more extreme successes and failures. This is fantastic training because you learn the most from your catastrophic failures and phenomenal successes.

 In every decision ask yourself what outcome would I regret. As you make proactive decisions and take positive actions, resentment turns into contentment.

Resentment of the past prevents us from feeling gratitude for the opportunities we do have. As we move towards gratitude, happiness and trust, others begin to trust and support us. This move is within our power. Belgin Irmak, Tax Advisory Senior at an accounting and professional services company, says that sometimes your situation isn't what you expected but you have to remind yourself that the outcome is in your hands:

> I completed my education in Turkey and was already well established. I then came to the UK, and had a tough time getting settled. I had to be really resilient and didn't give up.

Giving up the resentment might feel like giving up control, but in reality, gratitude is what gives you the agency to freely make logical and empowering choices.

Gratitude, and not resentment, puts you in charge of your own destiny. Giving up the resentment might feel like giving up control, but in reality, gratitude is what gives you the agency to freely make logical and empowering choices.

Migration wakes your dormant genes

When I was 10 years old and living in Iran, every Friday we used to go for a family walk to our local park. Iran as a Muslim country has Friday as a non-working day of the week. There was a stationery shop in a small portacabin selling all sorts of essentials for kids. I went in one day and saw packs of coloured paper. Each pack had 25 small sheets of paper in a single colour. I was disappointed that you had to buy 10 packs in order to get every colour. In that moment I thought maybe kids at school would be willing to pay me more if I gave them the choice. So, I borrowed from my father 10p in local currency which enabled me to buy 10 packs, one in each colour. The next day during school breaks I offered five sheets in any colours of choice for 1p. Despite the 400% profit I was making, the demand was so high that I had to get one of my friends who was taller than me to get the kids into a line. She said she would do it for free but I didn't think that was fair so I gave her five sheets in the colours that were left at the end of each day.

I remember this girl, who was often not nice to me, all of a sudden became very nice and the next day she asked me where I bought the supplies from. I could tell she wanted to steal my customers and I told her as much. You see, in Iran during the war it was a sellers' market so you had to guard your suppliers.

After a few weeks I got called into the principal's office for the first and last time in my life. I got a big telling off for selling things at school. I explained to her that I genuinely didn't realize this was not allowed and that I'd be really happy to share half the profits to buy supplies for the school. She did not look impressed and said that if I continued, she would have no choice but to mark me down for discipline and remove me as form captain. This meant a lot to me because to be declared number 1 in the school each term, you had to have the highest average score across all subjects including discipline. I immediately apologized and promised never to do it again. I kept my promise, as I always try to do, but I still remember that clear but bitter choice.

When I remember the early ambition and drive I had as a child, I occasionally wonder where would I have been if we had not moved to the UK. Would I have achieved more or less? Would I have been doing the same job or not? Would I hold the same views or not? I think, while some of the early characteristics I displayed would have worked well in either country, my migrant experience has shaped me. It is almost like my bones were broken and mended stronger. My eyes see things with multiple lenses. I see connections between variables and a path forward that others don't at first see. I certainly have more empathy, passion and drive. Migration causes a mutation, metaphorically speaking.

Daniel Khan, Head of Business Development at an investment management company, explained the

challenges his family have gone through and that this
motivated him to seek success:

> My father is Indian and mum is British. My
> dad was brought over at 18 months old by his
> mother; the family had problems and he was in
> and out of care. My mum and dad worked very
> hard and put everything into putting me into
> private school and this sacrifice and their care
> led to and drove my successes.

There has long been a debate about nature versus
nurture. I believe people rely too much on nature to do
the work for them. They blame their genes when they
don't achieve what they wanted to. Some think because
they seem to have so-called 'good genes', success is
automatic. I say to them, if you think you are a Ferrari,
that confidence is great but know one thing. That even
the Ferrari needs you to put fuel in it; if you don't, the
Ferrari is not going anywhere. Your decisions, actions
and hard work are the fuel. Even though migration
causes a mutation and changes you, you have to do
something positive with that change. You have to take
full responsibility for your life. It is one thing thinking
logically and attributing causes to what has happened in
your life, but it is another thing getting stuck in blaming
others. We are responsible for the way we respond to
events in our lives. I have noticed throughout my life

that this approach turns even the most adverse events into remarkably positive life outcomes, no matter how improbable that seemed at the time.

Everyone is gifted at least one thing. We call the successful outliers genius, exceptional, lucky and make everyone else feel ordinary and inferior. This is flawed and ignores what really ignites superior performance. Every 'extraordinary' person has had a profound experience that made them find their purpose, one person who helped them recognize their talent and changed their life, one opportunity that put them in the right environment and among the right people to nurture and support their dreams.

> Genes alone will get you nowhere. It is your character and life experiences that together ignite the unique extraordinary in you.

The good news is that anyone can do this because the biggest changes in life start with small steps and progress with leaps as we gain confidence and support. You need to learn about your own personality and how you perform at your best. You need to learn about others and what makes them successful and how you can contribute to that so you succeed with others. I am yet to meet a successful person who has done it all by themselves, and even if such a person exists, I think they would be lonely because succeeding with others feels so good.

Migrants often talk about their ability to fit anywhere. Mona Bitar, former Vice Chair UK and Ireland at a Big 4 accounting firm, described her experience to me:

> I came to UK for boarding school at 12 years old. My family is Palestinian and settled in both Jordan and Lebanon and even though they are highly educated, money for the school was tight due to the fact they had to flee their homes. They managed somehow. I then faced a visa problem which is one of the reasons I did a PhD and many had to support me financially. People mention how non-Arab/white I look and there was always a feeling that I neither fit in the Arab world nor in Britain which created a lifelong identity crisis which with age I have learned to deal with.

I said to Mona that we each get to define our sense of identity and heritage. Each person has a unique identity and their obstacles reveal their individual gifts.

Recognize your migrant magic

There has been so much focus on identifying our weaknesses and development needs. There are some cases where a weakness is so fundamental to our success and the wellbeing of others that we do need to address it. However, the greatest successes in life have come from identifying, developing and leveraging our greatest strengths.

So, what are the greatest strengths that migrants often have in common?

Before I tell you, I should say something. You have to embrace migrant magic for it to work. First, recognize that being a migrant is something to be proud of. You are a pioneer, an adventurer, someone who takes calculated risks to improve your family's life. Second, have belief and trust in yourself, in the system and in people. Have faith that if you are a decent person and that if you work hard and work smart, you will eventually get what you deserve. Last, don't blame others; empower yourself by believing that your destiny is in your own hands and that you have ownership of making your future the way you wish.

By embracing these principles, you will become one of the many who develop migrant magic.

Migrants don't go to another country to fail; they go to succeed. The deep desire to succeed and contribute is one of the key characteristics of migrant magic. What gives each of us that drive will be different. For me it comes from a place of love for this country that welcomed me. I want Britain to be the best that I know it can be and I want everyone in the country to prosper together and, yes, I want us to compete on the world stage and be among the very best in the world. I want to help create a Britain that my children will succeed in and grow up happy.

For others the motivation is to lift the next generation in their family out of poverty. They know that they cannot do that by relying on minimal benefits, and that they need to use education and hard work as levers of their family's social mobility. There is also a sense among most migrants that their move to a more stable country with established economic and social systems carries less risk relatively when you invest your efforts and hard work. Bilkis Shittu, Director and Founder at Clarified Accounting, has found that many migrants use that ambition to take calculated risks and start their own businesses creating jobs in their host country:

> I had my education in Nigeria, worked with a Big 4 accounting firm and was well established. I then came to the UK and worked with top firms. I did a conversion to ACCA and set up my own accounting practice. I feel motivated by my role in bringing my skills to this country, supporting businesses and creating jobs. As a black Muslim female, I hope that I can be a role model for under-represented young talent in the UK.

The Ipsos Nation Brand Index shows UK's perceived strengths in Science, Technology and Innovation. These are perceptions around the world about the UK, but we need to deliver on that perception in order to gain the economic and structural benefits. I was struck by the sense of pride I felt in Katrina Borissova, Director Strategic Planning Projects and Chief of Staff at a pharmaceutical company, when we met:

> I have wanted my contribution to be about innovation throughout my career. I am based in the UK and work for a growing bio med company headquartered in the US. I have worked at big Pharma for years and even launched my own vegan beauty products start-up.

This sort of innovation needs a resilient, proactive problem solver. I can see first-hand why so many migrants boost innovation in their host country through this particular source of migrant magic.

Sometimes you recognize your migrant magic through an everyday comment someone makes. I remember the first time someone in an open plan office kindly asked me if they were disturbing me with the noise, I smiled and said not at all. They couldn't possibly have known what my smile was really about. As I was growing up as a child in Iran, six years of that time was during the war, with bombardments on many nights. During those years I did much of my homework with candlelight in a basement full of cockroaches while the bombs were falling. I knew the danger, as I went to school each day wondering who would still be alive. If you can focus on homework under such circumstances, noise in an open plan office is not going to sidetrack you. This kind of super-productivity and mental endurance is characteristic of migrants coming from war zones.

> Know the value of your hardships. This is how you get to be introduced to who you really are and occasionally discover magic. Recognize the special talents in yourself and others.

Others discover this endurance during their adult life. As a mother I really understood how tough it was for Njideka Chima-Amaeshi, Doctoral Researcher at Newcastle University:

> I came to the UK with a job as an engineer. I had to work offshore in order to keep my visa and I was also doing my Master's at the same time. Then I got pregnant with my son and had to go back offshore after my maternity leave. The same as when I had my twins a few years later. Sheer determination is what got me through this time.

So, you have a deep desire to succeed, you are a resilient and proactive problem solver, and you are super-productive through your mental endurance. What more migrant magic do you need?

You need to bring others with you and succeed in groups. That is where migrants' cultural adaptability comes in. In the short term there are costs to migration and challenges in the local communities that migrants move to. But over time and in the long term there is a net benefit to the economy and society as migrants settle down and succeed in their host country. Alejandra Alvarez Pineda, Senior Medical Education Associate at a multinational medical technology company, explained to me how hard this cultural adjustment was at the beginning:

> I came from Colombia aged 12, with my younger brother. My mother had come a few years earlier as a refugee and we had stayed with my grandparents in Colombia. When we eventually joined my mother, we found the cultural aspects of fitting in here difficult. But by living our everyday lives we learnt to adapt culturally and I ended up being the first in my family to go to university.

This early challenge and experience in cultural adaptability often turns into a later strength. I could see how popular she was with a diverse set of employees as I walked through her office in London with Fationa Bejko, Partner Marketing Lead UKI at a leading global technology company:

> I came from Albania to the UK as an immigrant at the age of 15. I had to learn fast how to adapt and get on with a variety of people in my host country. The skills I learnt at that difficult age in a new country, really was the foundation of the marketing and partnerships professional I have become.

Fationa had such an interest in people, collaboration and connecting that even though I knew she was culturally adaptable to most people she met, she still made me feel special. That has got to be migrant magic.

Chapter 3

Drop your migrant saboteurs if you really want to fly

There have been some pivotal moments in my life where something has happened that others might see as inconsequential, but I felt in my gut it was going to define the direction of my life depending on what I did next.

When I started in GE, the business I joined as financial controller was newly acquired by GE. Despite my young age, GE had made it clear that I was their ally there and my job was to work closely with the business to integrate that acquisition. To align their business and processes to the GE way of doing things. On my first day, I introduced myself to my finance team, and five minutes later one of the key staff members came into my office and told me that she was almost twice my age and that she was not going to work for someone so inexperienced. It was as if time slowed down as I was listening to her. This was a pivotal moment. I realized her feeling was not unreasonable given the acquisition and that she wasn't entirely wrong about my lack of experience compared to her. I knew that I had two options. Either I pull rank and use the power GE had given me, or I talk to her like a human being and tell her what I really think. I remembered that my father always told us during our childhood that just because you have a power that does not mean you should use it without thought or measure. I said to her she was right. I was only 25 and that I really needed her accounting knowledge and experience of the business for me to do a good job. I did give her a little smile and told her she'd be surprised how quickly I learn. For the next six months, I hardly ever sat in my office; the arbitrary hierarchy was coming between us as a team. A few months later, together, we achieved the highest level in our GE internal audit and we celebrated as a team.

Next came the engineers. I couldn't really influence the outcomes for the business if I didn't get under the bonnet of operations. The lead engineer was a highly respected man and I went to see him one day. You could tell he thought a finance person had no place in the factory or in the R&D department. I asked him how I could help. He said it wouldn't make any difference because his views were no longer listened to. I told him that I grew up with a hardcore engineer father and uncles and that I knew his knowledge was why GE acquired this business. With his full blessing, I spent the next several months doing my financial controller job by day and my Six Sigma rep role with the night shift engineers. Through the projects we worked on, we gained much GE investment and the business became a regional centre of excellence.

People want to support you when you open your mind and heart

So, what has this got to do with migrant saboteurs?

I could have taken the view at each encounter that these people don't like me because I was different from them, but I didn't. If I had, I would have been plagued by some of the saboteurs that some migrants adopt. In this instance, it would have been the saboteurs of being super-vigilant and overly critical. The end result being you don't like or trust anybody and no one trusts you either. The best way of knowing who to trust is by trusting them after you check their intentions. Of course, you have to look for the signs of who is trustworthy and who has been reliable and honest with you, but do this with evidence rather than fear.

People want to support you when you open your mind and heart. Nobody in their rational mind would say no if you present them with a solution that benefits you both. Don't push people into a corner or hurt them, as they may then be driven by desperation and that is not in anyone's interest. As a result of this ethos, people who have supported me come from all walks of life and only have two things in common: their logic and the desire to succeed.

You are different but not that different. You can always find common ground with people. I remember my heart-to-heart chat with Sara Radenovic, Director Managed Access Programs at a FTSE 100 global pharmaceutical company, when she said:

> I am myself from Serbia, now living in the UK.
> I grew up while Yugoslavia was falling apart
> and war was everywhere.

When I first met Sara, I noticed she looked and sounded very different from me as an Eastern European female scientist. But the more we talked, the more I realized our hearts were connected as we both grew up as our countries were falling apart and war was everywhere. We truly bonded and opened our hearts. I knew in that moment why she was supporting Migrant Leaders.

There are more reasons today to revert back to the view that they are against us because we are migrants. I wouldn't blame you for feeling this way, but this thinking is not helpful to anybody. I remember speaking to a remarkable man, Nitin Parmar, Director Developer Relations at a global financial services company. He shared with me:

> I moved to the UK as a child with my parents
> and multiple siblings from Africa. We are
> of Indian origin. We lived in Tottenham and
> experienced a lot of racism and prejudice as I

was growing up. Recently I have been pulled back to that time and I feel that I want to share the knowledge of my successes. I want to give something back to the community based on that experience.

Migrants have a sense of purpose that if nurtured can create harmony in British society. Nitin has used that early experience in a positive direction.

Don't take the anti-migrant sentiments personally, there is something bigger at play. The anti-migrant sentiment today is said to be based on the view that migrants bring crime, terrorism or take our jobs. This is a fallacy. The facts and data don't support that view. People are feeling disillusioned, angry and fearful of a future where they will be poor in their retirement and their children may be worse off than they are. They need someone to blame and it's easier to blame the migrants than governments and multinationals across the world.

Right now, around 70% of wealth in the US is owned by the top 10% of society. Around the world half of the wealth is in the hands of just 1% of the population. This is the same sort of inequality as there was a hundred years ago when the aristocrats owned the vast majority of capital. What's more is that through industrialization, automation and deregulation, the way to build wealth is through capital rather than labour. For centuries the average return on capital has been around 5% and yet the growth in overall economies has been 2%.

For a while we felt better for the cheap goods we got to consume from China and the addictive habits soothing our worries. We have tried to balance the inequality by deregulating financial markets and providing cheap credit to everyone. But every time (and memories are short) the bubble bursts, who pays the price? Is it really the elite of Wall Street, the CEOs of Main Street, or is it the ordinary people whose homes get repossessed?

The long neglect of the working class has driven voters to political extremes. The two are playing political ping pong with the public and the migrants are left to be blamed in the middle of all this. I ask myself what is someone like Farid Froghi, Specialist Registrar in HPB and Liver Transplant Surgery, NHS, to do:

> I literally walked with my family to Germany from Iran and got into the UK on a lorry. I spent many months in police custody and refugee camps with my family. I ended up going to a tough London school and had to get help from another school to write my personal statement to go to university. Me and my brother Saied

were offered to be trained as labourers! But my parents insisted on us studying. We are now both surgeons and working together in the same hospital!

This reminds me that retaining who you know you are is so important. I say to young people who are going through tough challenges, you can put oil in a bottle of water and shake it vigorously but remember this, it is in oil's nature to rise to the top of the water in the end. Trust and work with your nature. You will rise to the top.

Trust your nature and let it do its job. You can put oil in a bottle of water and shake it vigorously but remember this, it is in oil's nature to rise to the top of the water in the end.

You have more capital than you think, so use it and share it

Sometimes mentees mention to me how unfair it all is that their family has no money at all and that having survived many things, they have to fight for the fees to go to university. Occasionally I sense resentment in their voices. I say to them, you have a secret capital that no one can purchase. Your culture is your capital. Your family's values are their most precious gift to you.

I remember asking my father when I was young, whether he ever resented his father for not understanding his vision. You see, when my father received the scholarship from that top technical university, his father tried to stop him going. Despite this, my father explained to me that he feels deep gratitude towards his father because his most valuable characteristics were learnt from him. He told me that his father was the hardest working man and he worked day and night on the farm to feed his family. He always liked to finish a job and do it to high standards. He wouldn't come to eat lunch unless that fence was fixed properly or another job was done. My father explained to me that the most important gifts his father gave him were his work ethic, his determination and discipline, his sense of duty to family and community. It was at that moment that I realized capital isn't really about money and resources. It isn't even just social capital and knowing how to behave and present yourself. We can learn that. True hard-earned capital comes from generations of cultural learning and heritage.

Regardless of your background your family have given you capital that money can't buy. Feel the advantage in that.

How you contextualize your situation really matters. Don't fall into some of the other migrant saboteur pits of becoming the victim who tries to avoid everything and blame everyone.

The evidence of family values shining through is abundant and I remember Parmesh Rajani, Head of Transfer Pricing at a FTSE 100 global retailing company:

> I grew up in Leicester with refugee parents who are Ugandan Indian Gujerati. We had absolutely no money but we were laser focused on education along with being part of a supporting, loving and nurturing household. That's why I went on to get a Master's in Economics.

This experience is replicated across the country and I have spoken to so many Migrant Leaders mentors, such as Nehal Rajnikant Jilka, Partner, at a Big 4 accounting firm. Despite his humble background, enterprise and ambition were integral to his family values:

> I guess my story begins with my father leaving Uganda and as a family living on a council estate in Birmingham; it then is about myself as the Indian boy from the corner shop to becoming a Big 4 firm Partner.

I am really proud of what migrants have achieved and I want us to share that capital with all others in the country who are being left behind. The human brain has such an impulse for either/or thinking. It is them or us. Evolution has given humans this ability for categorization that also divides us. Yet, the most powerful motivators are what experiences, fears and hopes we have in common that transcend those categories of people in society.

We also have a lot to learn from the others in the host country. As migrants we bring our diverse strengths and we need to leverage those abilities. But we should also notice what the people in our host country do well and learn and benefit from that. I remember a conversation about flexible thinking, with Sami Ben-Ali, Head of Diversity Recruiting Programs – EMEA and LATAM, at a leading global e-commerce company:

> There was no way of me studying back then without my parents taking on debt. Education was paramount and pushed my parents, especially my father as they believed it was the only way for their children to get opportunities. My father, a migrant who worked doing manual labour on farms, and my mother was also working class from Liverpool. If time went back, I wished we were more flexible and considered apprenticeships.

The cross-cultural learning benefited Trinh Tu, Managing Director Public Affairs at a multinational market research and consulting firm, who explained to me how proud she is of every culture she is part of:

> I am a first-generation refugee who fled conflict in Vietnam with my family when I was nine and was given refuge in the UK. And like many refugees before me, I have made the UK my home and I have fully embraced its values, culture, and opportunities. I have thrived in the freedom to pursue my education, to build a successful and rewarding career, to make enduring friendships and relationships and to have my own family. My birth culture is still very special to me, and it is something that I share with my children. But it does not define me or hold me back. I see myself as British and Vietnamese and I am very lucky to be able to be both.

As my father said when we entered the UK, keep the good parts of our culture and learn all the good parts of British culture.

You are destined to succeed and contribute to your host country

For one moment imagine that everyone wants you to succeed and is cheering for you. Imagine that there is no nepotism, no discrimination, that you are in a meritocracy and only limited by your own ambitions. Dare to imagine the future you could create for yourself and others when you believe anything is possible. It is empowering, liberating and motivating.

Believe in your ability to follow through with your purpose and make your dreams come to fruition. Even if this assumption is not realistic or true, believing that your future is determined by others who want to discriminate against you is not a helpful belief.

Believe in your purpose and ability and no one can stop you succeeding, no matter how biased, prejudiced or powerful they are. No one can stop your migrant magic. Rahul Welde has spent 30 years as a global Executive Vice President at a FTSE 100 multinational consumer goods company and he explains how his determination to take responsibility for his future helped him navigate a very different career from the one he had envisaged:

> Growing up as a child I was quite focused on becoming a pilot in the Indian Airforce, well into college. Unfortunately, that didn't materialize,

and I had to pull myself together. I learnt to accept and overcome failure, preparing myself for an alternate career. I learnt to bounce back, take responsibility and pursue another dream. As it happens, I made a success out of my corporate career, which provided me a strong foundation as well as my global home.

> Have strong faith in something. Build the belief that something bigger than you is supporting you and that you are destined to be happy. As you keep succeeding you will learn to switch on that belief and ability at will.

Others had to show remarkable self-belief when their family didn't share their ambitions. Alina Timofeeva, Associate Partner at a multinational management consulting firm, explains:

> I came from a disadvantaged background in Russia, and my family didn't share my ambitions. I have never let that stop me or my husband who came from India 15 years ago. I am more determined than ever.

Work hard, there are no shortcuts. But do be careful, there are migrant saboteurs lurking here too. Know the difference between being ambitious and a super-achiever who becomes restless or controlling. Humility is the new smart work. In the new machine age, your humanity is your advantage. This is not just for the benefit of others, but managing your own ego will benefit you more than anyone else. Leaving your ego at the door, you will also leave behind your insecurities and fears. You will see things more objectively, creatively, with hope and the courage to collaborate with people who may be different from you.

A paradigm shift is a decision. When I moved to the UK, I decided that I would immerse myself in British life with an open mind while remaining authentic to my ethnic roots and my personal character. I made that decision because I believed that was in my interest and felt that was the right thing to do. This decision got further embedded with every kindness, friendship and support I experienced from the British. It also meant I didn't let anyone racist, sexist or unkind, and I did encounter such people from time to time, destroy me. This shift in paradigm was a logical decision for me and I envisioned the end game.

But everyone is different. You need to find your buttons to press in order to make the paradigm shifts that are needed for success and happiness. And you need to do this as soon as you are ready to. The sooner the better. So, if you don't feel ready to, there are things you can do to speed up the shift. Widen your network and exposures to expand your thinking, get an inspirational mentor you can relate to whose success you would want to emulate.

Above all, choose the belief that you are destined to succeed. This gives you confidence to 'switch on' that ability. This particular paradigm shift needs psychological safety. You need to surround yourself with friends, mentors and a support network who will catch you with a safety net if you fail. It is OK to fail. I know I failed way more than once.

Chapter 4

Maximize your migrant success with intuition, analysis and flair

I remember a story my dad used to tell me about his village. He said that there were only two people in his village who could read and write. One was the mullah in the mosque and the other was my grandfather, motivated by his desire to be able to read the Koran.

You may think that because there was such poverty and illiteracy in his village, there was no wisdom. You would be wrong. He remembers one day sitting around the pond in the village and an old man approached him. He told my father that he had heard stories about him in the village, this boy called Ali who is so bright and determined. He told my father, you see this pond, that is our village and see the little fish in the pond. You are not a little fish; you are not meant for a small pond like this. You need to find your ocean.

That story guided me throughout my life and I remember when I was doing my degree in Hull, I used to cycle on Sundays to the Beverley market to buy good quality food much cheaper than any supermarket. The people were lovely, really friendly, and seemed quite well presented and posh to me. I heard that Beverley was where all the wealthy people retired to. I dreamed of one day being posh enough to retire in Beverley. But as luck would have it, work opportunities took me back to Birmingham and later to London. I would love to visit Beverley with my family one day, but I learnt not to make retirement plans too early. I now recognize that the extent of our ambitions may and should change.

When I was a young migrant in my teens growing up in Birmingham, I used to go to town most Saturdays and read in the library and look at the shops. Much to my father's dismay I often found Lycra dresses for just one pound at the bottom of cardboard boxes in Topshop. I also spent plenty of time in the shop called Game. My children now find it hard to believe that I was ever into computer games but I knew so much that customers in Game routinely assumed I worked there and I answered all their questions. One Saturday I heard a couple of the shop assistants talk about their hourly rate of £3.22. I somehow knew that the minimum wage for an adult was £2.74 at that time so despite their complaint of the low pay, I thought it was great and I asked the manager for a job. My pitch could have been better, because I told him I was now 16 years old, I knew all his products and the customers were always asking me questions. I was doing the job anyway so he might as well pay me a wage. To my surprise he agreed and asked me to work every Saturday if things worked out well.

This new-found success was important because this was around the time that we were supposed to have one week's work experience through school. I remember how my heart sank when I saw the printed list of work experience opportunities at school. There was nothing that would use my love of maths and science. Nothing that inspired me and nothing that I would be good at. I knew I wouldn't make a good hairdresser, butcher or other work roles they had listed.

I had just done my sociology GCSE project and had learnt about socioeconomic groups and how in Birmingham there were differences between Harborne and Bartley Green where my school was. So, I put on the best and most suitable outfit I could and went to Harborne High Street. I went door to door asking for work experience. They all said no, and secretly I was glad because they were all shops and I figured even with the staff discount I couldn't afford to buy anything anyway. There was hardly any benefit for me working there.

But then I passed the NatWest bank and I thought this could be interesting. When I was much younger, I used to sneak into high street banks and quickly take their free leaflets so I could read them at home. I knew I had some interest in banks even though they don't do science. But it was quite embarrassing asking them, so I hovered around for a while pretending to read the materials there. I must have looked uncomfortable because a kind customer approached me and asked if I was alright and she took me to the counter. I explained to the clerk at the counter that I was looking for one week of work experience and in truth I had nothing else to say as I had no idea what work experience actually was.

She arranged for me to talk to the bank manager and I told him how I was teaching maths to save money so I could buy the new Capital Bonds paying a guaranteed interest of 12% per year for five years and asked him if they had savings that could beat that rate. He told me he would see what they could do. I really had to hide my excitement and just show gratitude when he agreed to give me one week of work experience. It turned out to be one of the best weeks of my working life. I had a meeting with that same bank manager at the end of each day when I would explain to him what we had done that day, and he actually seemed interested in my ideas. They rotated me across different teams such as the cashiers at the counters, observing meetings, visiting multiple cashpoints and seeing what was inside them. They even trusted me to count some money.

It was the first time that it occurred to me that my maths could be useful in an industry other than engineering and science. That is probably why I chose A Level economics as a completely new subject to me, and discovered a new love.

That experience with NatWest really widened my horizons so now when I used to go to town, I explored outside the cardboard box in Topshop and Game. There was an area near Colmore Row where there were a few prestigious firms. I used to every week go and look up at the Ernst & Young building, wondering what kind of people worked there. I didn't even dare dream that one day that could be me. As it turned out, that would become me.

Find your purpose

I smile when people declare that they want to be a millionaire or a CEO by a certain age. They sometimes ask me how to achieve that. I tell them straight, that I like their ambition but to get there they must focus on another objective. If money, status and power are your primary objective, you will never achieve it. Even if you do achieve fame and wealth that way, you would have forgone the kind of leader you could have been. It matters how you win, so follow your purpose, not the money. The money will come simply as a by-product of the value you create. Know what value you create in any organization, learn to measure it against the organization's objectives and make sure they are fair to you. If they don't intend to be fair to you, get out fast and take your value somewhere else. There is no confidence class that will really make you believe in yourself like success. Achieve some early quick wins to boost your confidence and the morale of others around you.

Other times people make me smile are when they make career decisions based on marginal monetary differences between two job offers, when the real difference is the trajectory of each job and where it will lead. Decisions based purely on money will not lead you to the investment needed in skills, knowledge and relationships that create sustainable success.

> Money is only a by-product of success. Don't chase just the money. If you get the big picture right and do the work, the money will follow.

I said this to one of my mentees and, under-standably, given the hardship he and his family had gone through, he said that's all very well but we need food on the table and he never wanted his family to go through that poverty again. I get it. Maslow's hier-archy of needs. Which is why you can make money a secondary motivation and still fulfil your potential. You make enough for now to invest in the bigger prize later. But be prepared to redefine what that prize is, as I found out through my own rewarding experience with charitable work.

Career choices are sometimes a journey, as I learnt from a conversation with Sunny Deo, Strategic Creative Director at a leading global information technology and consulting services company:

I grew up in the north of England from a humble background. I started a Chemistry degree but changed my mind as I always enjoyed creative writing. In 2006, I found myself having to move abroad for work, first Dubai then Singapore, as entering the elitist London market was proving to be impossible for a BME aspiring to break into the creative industry. At the end of 2015, I returned to London with vast international experience, but still struggled to get noticed following hundreds of job applications. I therefore went freelance until July 2019, when my company saw how my accumulated international experience would benefit their new in-house creative team.

Others show such courage after a well-established career, and my friend Barbara Gottardi, former Chief Information Officer at one of the largest banking institutions in the world, and founder, comes to mind:

After spending more than 20 years in big corporates as CIO, I founded my own technology advisory business and I am launching a start-up. I want to make a difference and try to change the narrative making technology for positive change. I also feel I have been very fortunate and want to give something back where I can.

Finding your purpose is a question of strategy; knowing your greatest strength and taking it to a market that values that and whose stakeholders you care about. But above all else, stay true to your character. Farley Thomas, former investment banking Managing Director, and founder, always felt something was missing until he launched his diversity business:

> My family were migrants from India. I grew up with my mother who worked hard, including doing cleaning jobs. I ended up as an MD in financial services and then launched two coaching-related businesses afterwards to give back what I thought was missing in organizations.

There is no strategy book that will build lasting partnerships like personal integrity. It matters how you win. It matters to others and deep inside it matters to you and building lasting confidence in yourself.

A word of warning about purpose: not every job in your career will have all the intellectual and emotional fulfilment you wish for, use your best natural talents and earn you a fantastic lifestyle. The trick is to know the combination of those objectives that you need at various stages of your life. There is no doubt that being in a job and organization you believe in will boost your energy and creativity, and working with people who support you is key.

There is no networking technique that will make people follow you like credibility. To me, authenticity is key to credibility and trust, and my formula is about saying what you think, and then doing what you say.

Stay true to your character, if nothing else, no one can ever take that away from you.

Carve your path forward

I remember this *Harvard Business Review* article I read when I was at university, about analysis versus instinct. I am fascinated by how people ask are you an analytical or intuitive decision-maker. I am analytical because of the subjects I enjoyed at school and I am intuitive because my gut instinct has often proven right. The former keeps my hormones in check and the latter keeps my confirmation bias in check. Analysis and instinct are team mates and should be part of your toolbox. The art is knowing the combination to use in each specific situation.

As a migrant you bring a different set of experiences, perspectives and capabilities. The adversity you may have gone through has further revealed and elevated your gifts. This often gives you vision and instincts that others may not have. You will see opportunities, solutions and have empathy for others, which positions you for success.

Going through hardship heightens your instincts. From then on, encourage analysis and instinct to work together as your team mates.

But there is a catch. Having gone through change, adversity and possibly trauma as a migrant, sometimes your instincts hold you back because your fears are based on the previous environment and adversities you have experienced. Don't fear your instinct. Trust yourself but do bring analysis into your thinking, decisions and actions.

What does analysis mean in this context?

Listen to advice from those you respect and choose to trust. If you don't have a mentor, coach or advisors, you can network and find them. Look for multiple sources of evidence, data and also stories of how others have succeeded.

Every time we make a career or life decision, every time we judge someone, every time the stakes are high, we should use every means to check our intuition. Some decisions need analysis, evidence and deliberation. Some decisions need you to go further and consider the detail on how that would work in practice should you take that path. This should not mean paralysis by analysis, if you front-load the decision factors of most importance.

I wonder about the combination of analysis and instinct Alexandra Pluymackers, Principal at a multinational information technology company, used in carving out her career path. She had much to work out to find a profession for herself which was very different from her parents:

> I came to Europe as a refugee from Moldova with my parents. My stepfather was an engineer, but could no longer work in that field in Germany and my mother went on to become a medical assistant to help the family. I felt, that there is just no option to fail and I have to succeed with what I have in the new system. This attitude helped me to develop my career, working for global tech companies and today as an IT Delivery and Sales Director working with fashion and retail clients.

For others the stakes are high because of the weight of expectation from their families and themselves. Ade Onagoruwa, Head of Employee Relations and Diversity, Equality and Inclusion at a FTSE 100 property development company, explained:

My father was studying as a Printing student in London, but I was sent to boarding school in Nigeria, before moving back to the UK at the age of 15. This journey has made me highly driven towards ethnic diversity and social mobility. I have worked on many initiatives and always believe we should (and do) go further.

Remember that hardly anything in life is linear. Your path will work out as long as you work with the right principles, methods and people. When I graduated, it was the worst graduate recruitment year to date. On top of that I had other disadvantages such as my immigration status. I applied for 400 jobs and all rejected me. I filed all the letters in binders and called every switchboard asking to speak to the person or department the letter was from, just to ask for feedback so I could improve. I understood the practical difficulties of this when they said they did not provide individual feedback because of the high volume of applications.

I got one interview, though, with an accounting firm in Birmingham. It was literally a one-man band and at the interview he offered me the job on the spot. At first I was pleased and even the £6000 starting salary, way below then graduate salaries, wasn't going to put me off. I knew that building capital is not really about money. There was a deal breaker though. I asked him who I would be working with. He explained that he would be out at client meetings and I'd be expected to be at the office on my own to organize and tidy the paperwork. I asked, so who would I be learning accounting from, and he didn't have much of an answer. He told me I should be grateful for this job offer. I paused, one of those defining moments when time slows down, and said that I was grateful for the offer. I thanked him and respectfully declined.

I pressed ahead with more applications and got more rejections, and then there was a job offer. From a huge company and it was a proper graduate training role. I knew what a fantastic opportunity this was. But with a heavy heart I rejected the offer. The job offer meant I would have to move location. At the time my younger brother was living with me and was doing his A Levels. I really wanted to give him the stability that I didn't have when I was younger. As such, this wasn't a difficult decision and I didn't even mention it to anybody. I would choose family every time.

I have since learnt that those were the right decisions and that I made up for it by trusting my instinct and ability to forge a path ahead afterwards. I managed to find the critical path at every key decision point. I knew I had to because of all the disadvantages I had experienced. It is incredible what humans are able to achieve with momentum once we are on the right path forward.

Keep learning and refining your plan

Life is a decision tree; yes, you set your roots and foundations early on, but then have so many continuous choices about which branches and twigs to follow. As much as I believe hard work delivers magic, equally important are the decisions you make in life. Decisions supercharge your talents. Find what market you are a Ferrari in and supercharge it every day with purpose. Think of it this way: the Ferrari is your natural talent, hard work is the fuel, purpose gives you the motivation, energy and vision. Decisions are the map and the plan.

Refining your path forward is about widening your horizons to discover what suits you and then focusing and narrowing down the options to find the optimal path. This widening and narrowing of the span of your options continues throughout your career.

I have found that as my career has progressed and settled, the decision criteria have become more subtle. I have increasingly received wisdom by chance moments spent with people who may not have much status but who do have life experience and wisdom. About 10 years ago I went with an EY colleague, my dear friend Kamelia, on a London night walk for a homeless charity. We finished our walk through the night and got to the destination by 7am. We were shattered and hungry, so stopped at a terrace café to have breakfast. A man came over with a kind smile, he asked if we had done the night walk and thanked us. He explained that he had been homeless for decades, so I asked him to tell us more. He said it was a very hard life but on the positive side he had seen the whole country and asked us if we wanted to know what he does when he gets depressed. We said absolutely yes. He took two metallic spoons out of his pockets and did this fun song and dance for us. I couldn't help but notice how genuinely happy and proud his face looked. I thanked him for the nice conversation. In that moment that man taught me the power of perspective and joy, whatever your life situation. I now build joy as a criterion in every decision.

Absorb the wisdom of life from everyone around you. Life-changing insights could come at any moment from anyone. Listen to people.

Think of decisions as one of the ways you build your 'success reserves'. This is part of the capital you build which you will later use for your success. Decisions, focus, energy, healthy and supportive nurturing relationships help build your success reserves.

People say time and money are your most important resources, but in reality, it's your ability to use time productively that leads to success. That efficiency is determined by your energy, focus and health. The effectiveness and ability to scale that success are determined by your decisions, relationships, and longevity.

There is advantage in every situation, no matter how unfair or unfortunate a situation may seem. The key is to know that every time something doesn't go your way, you consider how you can extract advantage from this and get the final outcome to be better than it would have been for you. Tanveer Kaur, Manager, at a Big 4 accounting firm, achieved this:

> I grew up in Wolverhampton and my parents were migrants and worked in factories. It was really hard as they didn't have any career insights for me, but their hard work gave me the example I needed to be persistent.

Outsiders and those who have gone through hardship often display great courage, resilience and drive. They have something deep in common that you may not at first see. Emily Southon, Head of Financial Services Regulatory Law at a leading international bank, explained her background to me:

I was born in the UK but my parents migrated from Cyprus. I didn't have any direct mentors when I was younger in terms of my legal career and I had to work things out myself and persevere. My parents worked very hard to give us a good life. Ours is a really typical migrant family story and it gave me the drive to achieve my goals.

But migrants also sometimes have a disproportionate risk of being impacted by their past trauma and fears in a new, unfamiliar environment. Understanding how this could lead to some decision pitfalls not only mitigates this risk but could also be a tool for decisions that would fast track their success.

What if as an outsider, rather than constantly trying to fit in and mask who you are, instead you believe that your uniqueness is your differentiator? Your real competitive edge, your true contribution?

I recall coming to the UK at 13, going to three different state schools in three years, I had my fair share of racist comments from a couple of kids. There was a moment when I noticed that actually there were more kids at school who were intrigued by my differences than those who seemed determined to make me 'go back where I came from'. So, I decided to embrace my differences. Truly showcase them. It was scary but I was defiant. The haters used to call me a maths freak, among other things, so I did the opposite of what the racists wanted me to do. I helped any kid who wanted to do better at maths. They called me uncool, so I turned up at the school disco with my sunglasses on, fully strutting confidence I didn't know I had, on the dance floor. On other occasions they told me to go back where I came from, so I told them maybe we should ask the teachers who they preferred to leave this school. I got throttled and slapped in the face on my way home for that comment, so I told them I would tell the headteacher what they did, and they never touched me again. I knew what made me different and how it benefited me and others. I embraced it and earned more respect for it. The racists could no longer say a thing because my friends now stood up for me even before I could say anything.

This early experience triggered a method that formed part of how I bring value to every situation as an outsider, through what I would call 'continuous differentiation'. I ask myself in every situation: How am I different? What do I bring that will uniquely fill what is missing for this team? How can I help this project succeed spectacularly or this organization to grow exponentially? How can I compete with my own best? In my experience it is every team member's difference that contributes to remarkable success stories.

Interestingly, that joint success is the very thing that unites diverse people.

So once this 'continuous differentiation' becomes part of our DNA and we stop trying to hide our strengths in order to fit in, we divert our focus and efforts into doing this really well.

On my quest to recruit the first thousand mentors for Migrant Leaders, I discovered that other outsiders have also harnessed their differences to great success. This differentiation, coupled with the boost in determination and drive, meant that their experiences gave them migrant magic.

Chapter 5

Run the marathon that is success and expect a few sprints

Once I had settled down in my career and had two young children, I spent six years in London at News Corp turning around underperforming businesses with operational challenges. There were promotions I declined and external opportunities I didn't go for because I was really enjoying immersing myself in motherhood.

Then it was time to make the move I had dreamed of ever since I was a teenager, looking up at the EY office in Colmore Row, Birmingham. I wanted to move to the Advisory business of a Big 4 firm.

Challenges hardly ever present themselves at a convenient time. I knew this already, so when my son had a bad cold with a high temperature the night before my EY assessment day, I did what I always did, I slept next to his bed and looked after him through the night. By 7 am I was confident that he was going to be ok and I handed over to my husband and off I went for a full day of assessments at EY. I got to the EY office in More London Place in good time, grabbed a coffee at a nearby café and reminded myself what an opportunity this was.

When I entered the EY building, they directed me to a really nice conference room with breakfast laid out for us, and it soon became clear that we were three candidates for one senior manager position. This was the final stage of the recruitment process. I knew that it was going to be a group exercise, a partner interview and a presentation we had been asked to prepare for. I was well prepared but I was keen to assess who the other two were and how I could stand out. Straight away one of them commented how 'early morning' this assessment was, and I concluded that given what I had gone through the night before he clearly didn't want this badly enough. But I knew I had to focus and be at my best. The group exercise showed me that the other candidate was strong and we performed equally well. I knew that in my partner interview I would need to differentiate myself through my unique industry experiences because the other candidate had consulting firm experience and I had none.

Then there was another one of those meaningful moments when time stops. We each had to separately go into a room and present to a partner. I had prepared a bound pack which I held in my hand as I walked to the presentation room. It so happened that we passed the other strong candidate and he looked at my bound pack and he seemed really worried. He started shuffling his papers. As I walked away, time slowed down and I knew the job was mine to lose now. I was almost there. So, I focused and really enjoyed delivering the presentation I had prepared. After their short deliberation, they walked me into a room and I knew this was the verbal job offer. I knew what my salary negotiation strategy was, so I took a risk and asked for something else. I told them that I'd like our relationship to start based on trust and that even at this verbal job offer stage they needed to know that I had two young children and I would need client projects which were mostly based in London. They seemed determined to offer me the role and I was delighted. I rejected other offers, including one from industry with almost double the EY salary, and I have never regretted that decision.

People say life is a marathon, but I do believe there are also a few sprints in there. You have to know that life is full of challenges and be prepared to juggle, handle adversities and work hard.

Motherhood continues to be the most profound, rewarding and meaningful experience of my life. Everything I had always hoped and dreamed it would be and more. Equally it is the most challenging experience not just because of the inevitable juggling of managing career, kids and home, but because your kids are the one thing that you care most about. Whose pain you feel deeper than your own pain. The one thing that you want to develop, nurture and protect more than anything else.

So, when I say life is a marathon as well as a few sprints, I mean it, expect it. You are stronger than you think and the hard work and juggling are not going to break you. This applies to everyone: mothers, fathers, people with caring responsibilities towards their parents and grandparents, people particularly active in their communities. Life is a challenge for everyone and we have all evolved to survive it. The objective then becomes how to thrive in life, not just survive.

Put your purpose to work

I know several very special people and one of them is a female scientist, Ambily Banerjee, Global Head Clinical Development Equity at a multinational pharmaceutical company. She described her story:

> I grew up in India with loving parents. Moved schools for the first time in my life when we moved to the UK age 13. A few years later, felt like I belonged nowhere. I was a foreigner even when I went to my home country. I was stalked and harassed when I was a teenager. I knew I had to fight to survive but didn't have the strength of voice. I thrived at university, worked for a global pharma company for 14 years and finally learnt to fight for what I believe in.

What Ambily's sentiments remind me of is the importance of connecting with who we dreamed of being when we were young. These days I make myself accountable to my 10-year-old self. She had big dreams and gives me courage when I arrive at a crossroad.

I met Daniela Correia, Technical Sales Specialist Manager, at a global biotechnology company, in Cambridge. She told me that she has never lost her sense of adventure since her childhood:

> I came from Portugal with a Science background. In the UK I was a full-time mum for almost two years before deciding to apply to a sales role in a biotech company with my Science background. I think that spirit of adventure and trying different things before getting what you love is really important. I've recently decided to follow my heart and passion and to create my own business to help and support children and adults with their wellbeing and resilience.

> At times of confusion, ask your 10-year-old self who you are supposed to be. She had big dreams and knew what was right. Hold yourself accountable to her.

I remember playing as a kid, holding a friend's hands and then spinning in a circle, thinking this is inertia. Later on, early in my career really going for progression, sometimes I had the same sensation, feeling a combination of fear, excitement and that feeling of momentum. Throughout my career I called this 'the momentum test' to challenge myself towards roles that felt right and projects which needed that commitment and courage.

Sometimes we stop ourselves from gathering the momentum needed for success, because we feel like we don't belong. Hence, we think no one will support us on the way. We feel that there seems to be no one at the top of organizations who looks like us and no one who has gone through the same journey. I prefer to look at it differently.

There are micro-communities in every organization. I am not really talking about employee resource groups, but about how you can find your community within the organization and all around you. Find your community and you have found a family who will support you on your success journey. Your uniqueness is your superpower because you are the result of all the adversities, weird and wonderful things you have gone through as an outsider. This means you can find something in common with most people. They too feel like an outsider, hoping to connect.

To build meaningful relationships which you all benefit from, you have to start with the right intentions. If your only purpose is how the community benefits you, then it is not going to work. You need to value and celebrate each member of your community who is different from you in some way. This is not easy. Our brains have evolved to recognize difference and see it as risk. We have a tendency to surround ourselves with familiar people who look like us and think and say the same things as us. I always remind myself how it feels to be picked on, to be excluded, or singled out, so that I never ignore someone with alternative views.

You will find your way of building that supportive community. Dwayne Bonsu, Territory Manager at a FTSE 100 medical equipment company, told me the story of his mother being from Guyana and his father from Ghana:

> My Why is my ancestors who were slaves and made that treacherous journey. Many slaves died and were thrown in the sea. My father told me education is your way to progress. I grew up in Milton Keynes and studied Science. I want my daughter to feel she belongs and not to be discriminated against.

The power of creating such a unique community is that you feel safe to gather momentum, and to shine at your brightest, because you don't have to keep stopping to check if you fit in. Just like I felt safe to hold my friend's hands and together spin as fast as we could. When it comes to my community, you may be surprised to know that they span many ethnicities, backgrounds and socioeconomic groups. What we have in common is our purpose and the challenges we have all gone through. Our common experiences are thicker than blood or the colour of our skin.

Build momentum for a smoother ride

Momentum is not about creating an ocean overnight. Oceans are, after all, made of drops of water. Every big achievement is made up of small steps which then gather speed. I remembered this when I talked to Belen Solanas, Consultant Systems Engineer at a leading global networking systems and software company:

> My father was a farmer in Spain and didn't know anything about universities or companies. But he supported me and put everything he had into sending me to the US for my education. He knew that step by step things will be better for the next generation. I have had a great career as a systems engineer and find it very rewarding helping the next generation of girls in STEM subjects.

Big dreams and goals only happen because of the actions you have taken, and of course some support and luck help. People who have a positive growth mindset and an action plan tend to get more supporters and even luck seems to knock at their door more often. Don't feel daunted by your big dreams. Turn them into manageable components you must achieve, steps you must take, milestones to get to.

Above all, front-load the hard work if you want to gather momentum. If you have ever pushed a car that has stalled, you will have noticed how hard it is at the beginning. But once the car gets going, you just need a reasonable force to keep it moving. Momentum is like that.

There will be crises early on. Catch them and deal with them decisively. At the start of our lives the direction we choose is even more important than later decisions. If you imagine three people starting from the same point, but each of them moving forward in a different direction, the distance between their paths gets bigger and bigger as time goes on. You later see the results of differences in the right decisions and the momentum you gather. Someone who tackled the crises early on is Ritika Wadhwa, Chief Operating Officer at a consultancy, who shared with me her incredible story of achieving academic excellence and taking a direction that was not in line with her extended family's wishes at the time:

My immediate family (my parents) were open minded. They wanted the best for me, including an education and big career prospects. My father always encouraged me in every way, but he passed away suddenly when I was 17. Then the extended family and community took over. They wouldn't allow me to work and made my mother's life pretty difficult. I had to fight the patriarchy and do what I needed to do for my own independence and to create a life I visioned. What I was capable of was defined by society every step of the way. My gender, the colour of my skin and even my accent came in the way of what I wanted to achieve. I didn't let it though, as my purpose, values and vision were aligned. This is why I am where I am today.

There are often some difficult decisions to make at the beginning and you may feel like you are swimming against the tide. Tackle those issues decisively and with compassion and determination.

Momentum is about the right choices, and then having the discipline to implement those decisions with force, focus and pace. But it is also about flexibility. Having the 'hustle attitude' to explore new opportunities that are close to your heart and new ways of achieving your objectives. Follow your heart and then use your head to set the measurable goals, results and deadlines needed to gather pace.

I spent 25 years in large corporates learning all the skills and gaining the network which later helped me turn Migrant Leaders into the organization that it is today. If I had not been flexible, I may have lost my purpose and might not have launched Migrant Leaders at all. That adaptability may well mean that one day I come back full circle, bringing my now wider connections and what I have learnt, to help the corporates become sustainably inclusive.

People talk a lot these days about making mistakes, taking risks and failing. Don't misunderstand this. The value of failure is in the learning. But this doesn't mean you should close your eyes and have a go at anything with little thought for the decisions or planning. Don't shoot blind. The consequences of lack of analysis and poor decisions early in life can be seen in greater magnitude later in life.

So, the big decisions are important, but so are the small tweaks. Above all, implement all those decisions, big and small, with determination and momentum, because the one thing I cannot promise you is how long we are each here for.

 Once you have your strategy, switch to productivity mode. Front-load the hard work because life has more challenges in store for us all. You are no exception.

You may feel the stress of this, especially when you have many challenges overwhelming you. Learn how to compartmentalize and turn stress into focus. Know how much and when to use stress, like salt in a recipe. The right amount at the right time makes the recipe tasty.

Succeeding as a migrant feels like pulling away from Earth's gravitational pull. It feels impossible sometimes, with everything against you. Recognize that just like flying into orbit, it is difficult but not impossible. Put in all the seemingly back-breaking hard work at the beginning of your journey. You will make it, and once you are in orbit you will wonder how you managed to do what appeared to be the impossible.

Become that person as fast as you can

We all know people who spend their whole lives saying, 'I am going to make it big', 'I will be rich or famous'. There are two mindsets you should get right in order to be successful and, even more importantly, happy.

One is that becoming rich or famous should not be your primary objective. This is flawed and will not lead to happiness and sustained success. Follow your purpose, the big things that feed and nourish the person you are. The wealth and fame will come as a secondary by-product of your success. You may feel it's easy to say this when you have a roof over your head and food on the table and then some. As a migrant you may every day be trying to survive and provide your family with the basic needs. But your dreams, hopes and aims can still be directed at something bigger that represents who you are. Your challenges as a migrant don't define who you are and what drives your beliefs, motivations, strengths and unique abilities. I remember seeing a young Jamie Qiu, Founder and Director of EY Startup Accelerator, present a few years ago at EY. I recently spoke to him again and he explained his motivations to me:

> I am from mainland China and came to the UK with my family when I was 6 years old. I went to a state grammar school and was brought up to work hard and honour my family. Family legacy really resonates with me and I want to have impact in my life by doing things differently.

Mindset two is that thinking big will only lead to success through your actions and everyday behaviours. Behaviour is about what you actually do day after day, what I tell my children about 'everyday good discipline'.

It is this discipline and following their purpose that has led so many migrant families to success. When I met Bhavesh Mistry, Chief Financial Officer for a FTSE 100 property development company, at his office, I sensed that, and he explained:

> My parents migrated from India to the UK with the hope that it would provide more opportunities for their children and to make a better life for all of us. Neither had a university education – my mom worked on an assembly line, my dad in an engineering job. They made many sacrifices so my brother and I could pursue our education and careers. When I was still a young boy we immigrated yet again – this time from the UK to Canada as my father believed more opportunity existed there for our family. I studied hard, gaining a bachelor's and Master's degree in accounting and worked at a Big 4 accountancy firm. However, I was ambitious and felt there was more that I could achieve and so took a risk, moved to the UK and self-financed my MBA at London Business School. Since gaining my MBA I have worked in a number of progressively senior roles across consumer and retail industries, eventually securing a role as a FTSE 100 CFO.

Some people talk about wanting to succeed and how they believe they are a genius. I say to them if you believe you are a Ferrari, it is good to see that confidence and ambition in you. But remember even a Ferrari needs fuel and will go nowhere without it. Your hard work is the fuel you need. Don't rev the engine unless you intend to put your foot on the accelerator. Get that right as fast as you can. One of the best people I know who continually impresses me is Giovanni Sobrero, whom I met when he was a Production Manager at a luxury car company. His phenomenal rapid rise and career strategy moving up in engineering, production and operations has been great to watch. He is now embarking on his MBA at Imperial College. I regularly get messages from Migrant Leaders mentees Giovanni has helped to get into top universities.

> Become that person as fast as you can. The 'losses' will teach you and the early wins will give you much-needed confidence which will feed your future success and happiness.

A little warning about stubbornness versus determination. The difference is fundamentally about strategy and choice. The determined person has infinite power to change anything he/she chooses to. The stubborn person has no power because he/she doesn't choose what to apply his/her determination to. There is a silver lining. If you have been told you are stubborn, work on your thinking, decisions and choices and turn your stubbornness into determination.

This is important for migrants in particular because often we come from countries which are under-developed, developing or troubled, and strong stubborn characters were often rewarded. We have watched our parents succeed with that characteristic, but we need to refine and adjust this in order to succeed in developed countries.

The question then becomes how to maximize the impact of your hard work and determination. I feel that I have been climbing what I call a 'productivity maturity curve'. Early in my life I thought success was a function of talent and the hours you put in. Then I discovered it is also who you work with and the energy a sense of purpose gives you. Ultimately came an awareness of how you can maximize your outputs and outcomes with good health and personal contentment.

The bottom of that 'productivity maturity curve' is how you spend your time, then how you spend your energy. As you climb the curve it becomes about what occupies your mind, then what satisfies your heart.

You could be in a role that pays your bills so the most you will achieve is giving your time and energy. You may need the money, status, approval, so you focus on that role and keep your mind on it. But when the role matches your purpose, you give it your heart. This matters to productivity because it is with our heart that we take a leap of faith and persist when a work problem seems impossible. It is with our heart that we care about the results so much that we go to bed with it on our minds and we wake up with the solution. It is with our hearts that we collaborate and transfer knowledge to our colleagues simply because we care and want that organization to succeed, even long after we have left.

Always have a sense for the signs of where on that maturity curve you are in your current role and organization. Know how to press your own productivity buttons that would benefit your current organization. If your contributions aren't appreciated, know when to leave.

Life is unpredictable. Those with a plan might calculate what they need to do and by when in order to achieve what they plan to do. But there are two principles here that are key to success for migrants.

Recognize that as an under-represented group you will likely face greater barriers than most other people. So always be ahead of the curve in delivering on your plans. If you think you have to put in a certain amount of work to achieve a target, do it faster and put in more effort to make the results impactful.

In the history of civilizations to the present day, the poor and unfortunate have often been vilified as perhaps having inferior character or being born with lower ability, 'destined' to accept their fate. Migrants are one of the prime recipients of this injustice. Eject this thinking from your mind. Adopt a 'growth' mindset rather than a 'fixed' mindset and know that you are special, really special.

Chapter 6

Elevate others on your journey to multiply your magic

When I was about 17 years old there was huge pressure to fit in. I never cared about being cool but I started to get interested in wider things such as looking good. Comments from school kids added to that pressure. I remember I had bought a couple of what I thought were very good quality hairbands reduced to 10p in some shop. I used to judge clothes' quality the way my father still does, by checking the materials and stitching, not really considering brand or fashion. I wore them like an Alice band and as I walked into the sixth form common room, in front of everyone this girl shouted, 'What the hell are you wearing on your head?' I was so embarrassed, for once I had no answer. Some years later I realized those were tennis sweat bands.

I soon succumbed to my desire to improve my fashion image and I am ashamed to admit I kind of cheated. There was a dress that was already 70% off and Topshop had just advertised a further 20% off. Those days most shops were quite basic at their tills and shop assistants entered discounts manually. Knowing perfectly well that the extra 20% discount was only worth another 6% off the original price, I went to the till and I asked the assistant whether that meant 70% plus 20% so 90% discount. She said yes, and I bought the dress at 90% discount straight away. I was pleased to have the dress at a price I could afford but I felt terrible. I wondered if the assistant would get into trouble for making that mistake. I considered going back to say I made a mistake with the price but then I thought, if I do that, we would both get into trouble, so I decided against it.

This and other experiences taught me an important lesson in what my personal values are and who I am. I didn't like winning something by cheating. I vowed never to do anything like that again and to always negotiate hard but with honesty.

When we were younger my father used to say it is better to achieve this much with integrity than that much, showing with his hands a higher level, without integrity. How you win matters.

It also feels even better when you win with others. There are so many so-called leaders who talk about and even publish books on deal making, competitive advantage and winning.

What many don't realize is that real power doesn't come from having more macro-level money, position and status than others. It comes from the micro-level relationships you have with people. The test for me is do I have friends, colleagues and followers who believe in me and my abilities so that even if I was penniless, they would still run to help me when I hit a problem. In return I would and always have done the same in those trusted relationships.

What any human being needs is a few people who appreciate and understand them, who support and listen to them. That is the minimum standard for building relationships that are fulfilling for everyone. Do this, create 'collective value', share the credit in an equitable way and you will have an abundance of supporters.

Be selective about who you work with

In Persian, they say, 'Tell me who you live with and I shall tell you who you are.' They say this in the context of your choice of friends and I should say it sounds better in Farsi as it rhymes of course.

When Migrant Leaders students tell me about our corporate connections wanting to work with them, I tell them not to get too excited. I explain that they are more special than they realize and that actually the selection decision is equally in their hands. I advise them to select the right opportunity based on all the tangible rational factors I have taught them but also based on the company and people they believe in and want to work with.

Relationships are the greatest accelerator of success. Your time, energy and focus are precious. Shared values multiply the impact of success. A word of warning: where you don't have common values, this destroys any common objectives and capabilities you may have.

> Relationships are the greatest accelerator of success. If you don't have common values and objectives don't get into that relationship. It will only end in tears.

So how do we know which relationships to pursue and invest in?

My quickest formula for this is to watch out for signs that tell you whether you have shared values, common objectives and complementary capabilities. Do this without relying on people's seniority or status; leadership qualities and potential exist among all groups and levels in society and organizations. Identify them without judging people or being too rigid. I have learnt that the difference between so-called good people and bad people is not whether they would do wrong or not. The difference between them is quite how much pressure they are willing to take before they do choose to do wrong and, when they do, whether they learn from it and never repeat the wrong again. Yes, good people sometimes do bad things, but with support and self-awareness they do learn from it. Understand their values and motivations to bring your allies together.

I remember a conversation with Alpesh Mistry, Sales Director at a multinational brewing company, and thinking this is someone who is willing to step outside his comfort zone and do the right thing:

> My parents came from India and Kenya and I was born and brought up in Rugby, UK. There have been many cultural influences in my life and when we had our three kids, I didn't hesitate to take shared parental leave for my third child, the experience really allowed me to learn the day to day challenges and support my teams in the future.

Ashrina Parmar, Senior Director Global Change Management at a FTSE 100 medical equipment company, reminded me not to put people into superficial boxes:

> My migrant parents worked hard seven days a week, to give opportunities to their kids. With my family name being Patel, we are known for owning shops and working very hard. In my career, I took the qualities and values my parents role modelled and did something entirely different, making use of the opportunities they gave me.

Common values bring together many people of varying backgrounds. Often hard-working migrant families put their everything into the education of the next generation. They are not privileged, they are driven.

But drive and hard work, though essential, are not enough. Above all else, value supportive people on your journey. People are often puzzled by how ethnic minorities are so under-represented in senior positions across all arenas, including the corporates, despite their remarkable academic achievements and drive. In my view many of the initiatives and studies don't go far enough to measure and push for ethnic minorities progressing beyond senior executive roles. They are a step in the right direction but we need more sustained momentum in areas which address the root causes of the disparity, not just the quick wins that shift the numbers somewhat. One of the many contributing factors is that ethnic minorities are over-mentored and under-sponsored. Supportive relationships and influential stakeholders who would mention you, vouch for you and stand up for you at critical tough decision points, are an absolute must for career progression.

Similarly to mentoring, sponsorship of others can start early on your own journey and brings significant benefits to you also. So, get into the habit of identifying peers and others you'd like to mentor and support. This helps build trust in yourself, which is the first step in others trusting you. Honour what you promise yourself every day so that others can trust you.

So how do you find yourself sponsors?

True sponsors are willing to use their political capital for you. They are willing to risk their reputation on you. But don't expect this. This special position of trust, much like respect, is to be earned not demanded.

 You need trusted mentors and sponsors to succeed. This special position of trust, much like respect, is to be earned not demanded.

Instilling trust in others is the one competence that transcends all other abilities. You could be the most technically gifted person but if others don't believe they can trust you, you would not succeed on your lone journey.

People often associate trustworthiness with honesty and that is an important aspect. There are other essential components of trust though.

You need to keep working at building a track record of delivering results, which says you are credible. The results should be relevant, measurable and should be focused on things that matter to you and others. If you can link your results to the result others are seeking to achieve, then even better.

You have to do this consistently with competence, reliability and authenticity. That's why it is important to pick roles that leverage your natural talents, because the deep level of competence it takes to deliver results and make a career out of it is astounding.

Reliability is to do with your sustained ability to keep delivering those results. It is about you being a safe pair of hands and predictable. Yes, being predictable is good and the only good surprise is when you achieve beyond expectations. Reliability is partly the everyday practice of keeping your commitments. It is also when in the tough moments you show your intentions to stakeholders and demonstrate how you view your joint goals by not giving up and delivering through laser-sharp focus on the results that matter to them.

There is no networking technique that will make people follow you like credibility. To me authenticity is key to credibility and trust, and my formula is about saying what you think, and then doing what you say. It sounds simple but if you do that consistently with everyone, regardless of their status, then people will trust you and you will be proud of yourself.

Ironically, to instil the trust of others in you, you need to be open to trusting others. You have to be both trustworthy and trusting. This is sometimes hard for migrants because, on their journey, some authority figures and others may have broken their trust. Keep an open mind and open heart and perhaps assess the trustworthiness of others in exactly the same way that you are building their trust in you. Through delivering results with competence, reliability and authenticity in your intentions towards them.

Compete without destroying value for others

I really enjoy watching teenage high school movies and series with my daughter. There seems to be a common pattern in the plot with the straight A student either getting involved with the wrong influences or forming a vendetta against someone who has bullied them or done them wrong. It usually ends in disaster with everyone suffering and everything crashing and burning. I know these are just movies, but I bet you have, just like I have, been in such a situation where you have the choice to destroy your opponent or to focus on your own objectives and let the chips fall where they fall.

 Forget the idea of the zero-sum game. More collective value is created every day delivering on win-win scenarios. Build this into everything you do if you want optimal outcomes for you and others.

The instinctive assumptions we make in life really influence the approach we take in problem solving. In my experience of life there aren't many genuine zero-sum games. Where if one person wins the other has to lose. Yet quite frequently I observe people assume this automatically and destroy value for themselves and everybody. If for a moment they look for win-win scenarios, they will see that this is the space where most optimal solutions lie. In fact the 'sum' is not fixed either. You can together increase the value of the sum by the way you behave towards your opponent, which in turn influences their reaction to you. This brings you some surprises as well in the friendships you end up building with your opponents and the trust and respect that creates. An example of this is when we are told migrants are taking our jobs. That is not how the economy works. Every time there is a tech job unfilled, that is lost economic value. Every time there are backlogs in the NHS, education, infrastructure because there aren't enough essential workers, the economy's structural problems impact growth in all sectors. Every time we know the UK can no longer compete globally on cost and we need to innovate, we hear of a migrant family's unique take on solving a problem and entrepreneurial success. When migrants succeed, we all succeed. They concurrently will feel productive and valued members of British society, thereby boosting social mobility, tackling discrimination and strengthening communities.

Life is a collection of win-win games. Do it this way and you will expand what I would call 'collective value' for everyone, and through the trust you build, your share of the win. Get used to measuring the success of your decisions, actions and results by measuring collective value. You can tell people who don't do this because they do come across as self-serving with no intention of helping others.

I remember Aimée Dushime, Deal Advisory at a Big 4 accounting firm, and how early on her journey she wanted to contribute to others:

> I have been in London since 2021 and my country of birth is Rwanda. I'm a product of great mentors who have held my hand throughout my career journey. As such, I would like to pay it forward by mentoring other young people who are at the start or yet to begin their careers.

When you make decisions and are putting effort into something, don't just think, what is in it for me? Yes, think of the value it creates for you but also the value it creates for the people around you. For your team mates, your department, your company, your boss. Help others succeed in their objectives and always create value for yourself and others. Even for your competitors.

But what if a competitor doesn't operate in the same way as you? I have learnt this through experience: don't compete or work with people who don't share your values. Compete in markets that you are going to be the best in and that reward your mode of operation. This is one of the reasons why it is important to speak to mentors who work in the industries and companies you are considering.

> Find markets, companies and people who work well with your life philosophy and approach. You will be surprised how much more you can achieve when you feel psychologically safe.

What if a potential collaborator has resources and offers you riches and fame but does not share your values? Run a mile, as that will never end well.

I remember my father explaining to me that I should help my competitors at school do well. I asked him, what if they then do way better than me? He said that would be great because that will motivate you to push yourself to surpass them which will then in turn push them to surpass you. That way, step by step you will all become the best you could be. I have adopted this 'collaborative competition' all my life and the cherry on the top is that you have a north star that helps you feel happy, confident and at ease with yourself.

I had such a competitor when I was around 11 years old and still living in Iran. She was the only pupil at school who could beat me in science, and by a clear margin in biology. In turn, my maths was better than hers. I am sure she felt what I felt. Confused between mutual respect and envy. I decided that there was a potential trade here. So, I asked her to bring me any maths topic she was finding difficult and I'd happily explain it to her and we would do a few practice questions together. Gradually she opened up and I asked if she could do me a favour and we could explore biology together. We ended up spending the whole academic year thoroughly enjoying each other's company and became best friends. Needless to say, we both rocked biology and maths at the end. When I moved to the UK, missing her was one of the few things that brought tears to my eyes.

Win their hearts first and then their minds

During my childhood my father always said if you are talented and work hard then you will fulfil your potential. He wasn't wrong, but there is more to it than that. There is a cultural perspective to this, in part determined by the regions we come from. In the developing world technical abilities are highly prized because that's what they need to build industries. In the developed world this is still essential but not enough. There are more nuances, and other competencies enable and extend success, such as marketing, finance, robust governance. Building capability is like building a house. Without the foundations you don't have a house. But no one is going to buy a house with the best foundations if the other necessary fixtures such as windows and finishing touches are missing.

I see the success curve as an exponential curve. One that as we climb, the technical foundations and hard work are essential but only take you 30% of the way to the peak. The remaining 70% can be reached through acceleration by differentiating yourself and maximizing impact. That takes a different frame of mind and set of skills.

When you get to the top of that curve and you look across the horizon and reflect back on what got you there, you realize that actually you couldn't have done it without having the final ingredient: influence. It is this ability that sees individuals such as Javid Hamid, Partner at a Big 4 accounting firm, reach those heights:

My parents were both refugees following the partition of India/Pakistan and came to the UK shortly after. They both worked in factories all their working lives and had little money. I didn't go to university but with hard work, and some luck, built a successful career which has led to me now being a senior partner in a Big 4 firm.

The power of connection comes from really caring about what the other person's heart needs and not just what you think their mind wants. Win together, win their hearts and minds. People often ask me, how do you persuade so many people to support you? I always say, it's not about me, it's about them. I have followed this formula all my life. Ask not what they can do for you but what you can do for them. Whatever initiative you are working on you can often find a common space for both parties to collaborate and win together. If you can't see that common ground even after exploring, then don't waste your time and their time; disengage. Highlight and deliver on the benefit case for them straight away and they will support you. Once you work together and collaborate and they can then see the real benefits of your initiative, then you have won their heart and mind. Find the common ground that gives them what their heart desires, and then deliver on the business case that wins their mind.

Building strong relationships is a combination of chemistry between people and good, old-fashioned reliability and honesty. Say what you think and do what you say.

Their hearts may desire progression, recognition and glory, security or control. These tendencies have genetic roots which have become traits due to early life experiences. These emotional needs are embedded in us all. I really felt connected to my dear friend Wincie Wong when I first met her many years ago, and fate keeps bringing us back together. So, look beyond their titles and current lifestyles. There is a human underneath, yearning to connect with the experiences of their younger self:

> My parents were non-English-speaking immigrants from Burma, where I grew up in the United States. My mother was a garment worker and told me that computers would take over the world. When some enterprising Chinese immigrants set up computer classes in the empty warehouse next door to the factory, she enrolled me as both a form of childcare and a way to prepare me for this tech powered future. Along with spending every penny they had to buy our family a computer, this helped ignite my passion for technology.

It is helpful to accept that different people are at different stages of life and needs. You need to give them both intrinsic and extrinsic motivation. The intrinsic motivation, for instance, is the inherent satisfaction it gives supporting a young person and seeing them succeed. Extrinsic motivation, in contrast, relates to some other satisfying consequences which tend to be short term in nature, such as money, awards, social media recognition. I remember talking to Mary Carmen Gasco-Buisson, Chief Marketing Officer, at a leading global jewellery brand, who explained to me her motivations in supporting our Migrant Leaders cause:

> I am an immigrant and daughter of immigrants myself. In fact, the last three generations of my family have been immigrants to different places, so this is close to my heart.

To gain more supporters we need to recognize that people are at different stages in what I would call their 'cycle of needs' and that sometimes we have to give them the glory they need in order to open them up to more intrinsic rewards and contributions. You cannot blame them for their human needs.

Give them what they need upfront if you want an ally. Don't be so afraid of them breaking your trust. Eight out of ten times this approach creates the deepest connections and most collaborative working relationships. One out of ten times there weren't enough common objectives to create value. Finally, one out of ten times they do betray you. But at least this way you have tested the relationship early on and you failed fast and cheap. The best way to know if you can trust someone is by trusting them.

Power is ultimately what everyone is trying to gain. Because it gives us security, desirability, consumption, connection. It is the manner in which we each choose to gain power that distinguishes us. You don't have to destroy value for your competitors for you to win. When negotiating, some people resort to taking everything they can. They put a disproportionate amount of effort into taking a bigger share of the pie, when in reality they should have focused on making a bigger pie for everyone. This waste of focus and resources destroys value. So, as well as looking at what is valuable to you, understand what is of value to others.

There is so much emphasis on what tangible things each party brings to the table. Alignment of objectives and capabilities is essential but not enough. You need your relationships to click in order for magic to happen and for everyone to bring the best out in each other.

Chapter 7

Your host country needs you to succeed and give back

Migrants tend to come from less economically advanced countries where there is political unrest, inequalities and lack of opportunities. It is incredibly empowering to come to a country with opportunities and resources. I remember by the time I was 14, I was really keen to absorb everything I could learn in this country. I mentioned earlier that I used to go into high street banks and collect their leaflets about their customer products. I could not believe that in this country they give you those leaflets for free. I used to read every word in the leaflets and then listen to the evening news on TV to make sense of what was happening in the economy. I must admit that at that point what drove me was the purely selfish desire to be curious, learn and succeed.

Young people and others talk about wanting to change the world and to have social impact and help people. In my experience the passion for helping others is not enough if you want to help many. You need to have the get up and go to succeed yourself first, before you can give back.

One of the fundamental things I agree with my father on is in relation to our role in the UK. When we came here in 1986, I remember he told us that this was the land that started the industrial revolution and that the British were known for their culture and values. He said, they are good people and you must work hard and contribute to this country. This is now your community that you live in and you have duties and obligations towards them.

 Ignite the sense of common national purpose and service in yourself and others. It is energizing, positive and you will never feel alone again.

To this day I believe this attitude and belief have given me an open mind and heart. The British, from all walks of life and backgrounds, have really supported me throughout my life. I will never forget that in my toughest personal moments, with all the upheaval I experienced with my family breakup and migrant problems, my friends were really there for me. Yes, there was the occasional racist making terribly hurtful comments at school, at university, at work; a racist person has always been there. But I decided that in comparison to all the love and support I had from my friends and colleagues, the racist person is statistically insignificant.

I eventually had my revenge on the racists, because the best revenge is success.

Even in your reaction to someone treating you badly, do not destroy the other person; focus on your own and your allies' happiness and success. Some people may consider this a collaborative female approach rather than a competitive male approach. I find such stereotyping unhelpful. This is not a question of female versus male style. I assure you it is the logical approach, which creates significantly more collective value for you and everyone in the world.

Migrants have the drive and resilience to grow the economy

You may be tempted to get into your political camps and not see the bigger picture. Populist parties can shift the political centre – but we can, and must, move it back to an equilibrium that is equitable for all. The test of that equilibrium for me is equity through genuine opportunities, so that anyone with hard work should be able to achieve anything they set their mind to.

There is a public perception that immigrants from outside the EU take more out of the welfare system than they contribute to the public purse. This is incorrect. The research carried out by Oxford Economics on the fiscal impact of immigration on the UK, and by the Centre for Research and Analysis of Migration at University College London, suggests that immigrants to the UK from outside the EU make a net fiscal contribution of about £5.2 billion, thus paying around 3% more into the system than they take out. Many come here determined to succeed and contribute, despite the challenges. Emmanuel Nzolantima, PMO Lead at a Fortune 500 real estate company, explained:

> I first moved from my home country, the D.R. Congo, to South Africa and then to the UK to complete my Master's degree. I wished I had a Migrant Leaders mentor when I moved to the UK to help me establish my life and career. The journey to settle and get on the success path was not easy but it makes me determined to contribute and share my experience with other communities.

Your representation across key sectors matters. Democracy isn't just about votes, importantly it is about real representation in key sectors such as the legal profession. We have a responsibility to make sure we succeed and truly represent the multiple groups we each belong to. Whether immigrants, ethnic minorities or the working class. Faiza A. Khan, Legal Consultant, exemplifies this representation:

> I entered the Bar in 2021 and I am considered a migrant advocate and myself Pashtun. The journey to get here has been difficult and I know what this means for representation in the legal profession.

Given the success that populist parties have had in recent years, the old established parties even across Europe have arguably encouraged and adopted some populist policy stances. This is at a time that economies have gone through global shocks on top of the usual cycles, increasing people's tendency to blame their hardships on migrants. But migrants are not the problem, they are part of the solution.

As migrants we must focus on our success and contributing to our host country. When I came to the UK, I felt proud to note that I had moved to a country that was the fourth biggest economy in the world, with a thriving financial services sector and industry. I feel sad when I see that we are now the sixth, going down in a relatively short space of time. When I look at the root causes of lack of economic prosperity and inequality, the indicators are not moving in the right direction. The recent Goldman Sachs study into social mobility highlighted that the UK is near the bottom of the international league table for developed countries in relation to social mobility and equality; only the US and Switzerland have lower social mobility than the UK.

We can change this. Britain is the ship we are on for our life journey now and we cannot let it sink, even if the captain is partying below deck and encouraging the crew to do the same, while blaming the passengers. The good news is that as migrants we have the exact abilities, resilience and drive needed to turn around any trend and get the ship to its destination.

 We are all responsible for the continuing success story of this country. Ask yourself, what do I want to tell my grandchildren about what I did since coming to this country?

Whether immigrant or born in this country, we have the same objectives. To succeed individually and to grow Britain through social mobility. Don't take short-term negative sentiments personally. Know that in the long term your contributions to Britain and friendship with the British will prevail. Don't let the politics divide the nation.

It is rewarding to align your success to your host country's. But succeeding on your own is not going to be enough. We live at a time when the root causes of inequality mean that underprivileged graduates earn half the starting salary of privileged graduates. This is even before I mention regional disparities across the UK. We each need to succeed and then elevate many others after us. Preetam Singh Heeramun, R&D Technical Lead at a global leading company in air traffic management, has that empathy for Britain:

I came to do my degree in the UK 23 years ago and stayed. I really believe young migrants come with abundant social and intellectual capital to further their education and, in many cases, settle here. They strive to achieve and contribute to the UK economy and communities. I have since worked on ERGs, reverse mentoring and mentoring circles in multiple companies and I want to replicate that contribution in communities.

Migrants know and value the opportunities and security that their host country brings to their new lives. This enables them to take more calculated risks and create businesses and new career paths. The better infrastructure in developed countries allows migrants to be more productive and to settle down. They often take jobs that are tough, low-paid – jobs that no one else wants to take but essential to the efficient functioning of the economy. Other migrants actually come with high professional skills in the industries we have gaps in.

I had a great conversation with Thomas John Sebastian, Chief Executive Officer at a global IT services company, and his key point was how you can boost your host country through the industries of the future:

I grew up in India and Malaysia, worked internationally and then moved to the UK in 2012. When ethnic minorities reach senior roles in corporates it gives hope to young people, regardless of differences in socioeconomic background. Most of my family have a background in education and I had excellent corporate support throughout my life, so I feel compelled to help ethnic minority youths as the next generation of talent. Such push for diversity boosts British innovation, new industries, and economic growth.

To gain supporters for Migrant Leaders, I have had over a thousand meetings since I launched the charity in 2017. In conversation with many refugee charities, we talked about how migrants fill the skills gap in the NHS and IT sector. One told me that with £300,000 charity funding they get 12 refugee doctors into employment, a cost of £25,000 per doctor. It costs Britain £500,000 to train each home-grown doctor and, importantly, the current skills gap means that there are vacant positions, impacting the growth of our economy.

On the one hand migrants do bring short-term costs to local communities initially, such as housing, education and health. On the other hand, research shows that in the long term the net benefit of migrants to the host country is positive. However, this positive impact is eroded by the negative psychological effects of migration on the migrants themselves. So, if we think logically, we should be supporting migrants to feel welcomed once they are here and to fulfil their potential so that together we grow the economy for everyone's benefit. The adversity has further clicked something in them, something magical, which gives them incredible drive to succeed and prove themselves in their host country. If we give them a chance, together we will grow the economy for everyone's benefit. We need to grow the pie first before we argue about how to divide it. Imagine if you were in a kitchen fighting about the cooking of the pie and excluding people who could contribute but who need to eat, you would end up with no pie. How does that benefit anyone?

But this is not just about today, it is also about the future of Britain and our competitive advantage. We are not going to compete with China and India on cost. We need to compete on knowledge, innovation and talent. This needs fresh thinking, ideas and new ways of solving problems. Migrants come from such diverse backgrounds and experiences that their wide perspective and exposures can help unlock this competitive advantage. This is further fuelled by the drive that migrants tend to come with to succeed, prove themselves and contribute to their host country.

We should see migration as a strategic tool to grow the industries of the future and gain competitive advantage for Britain.

Divyesh Bilimoria, Director at a Big 4 accounting firm, and founder, described his refugee story:

> I was a child refugee in this country when thousands of Asian families fled Uganda in 1972. We had to start from nothing after initially being housed in a refugee camp. I recognized the opportunities in the UK after graduating from Imperial College.

The tough experiences that many migrants go through give them the drive to succeed, and through their success, they grow the British economy. Many I have spoken to talk about not wanting to ever be poor or unsafe again.

As my father said when we came to the UK, we must work hard and succeed in the UK because if you are going to be poor in your own country or poor in another country, best you are poor in your own country.

Use your magic ingredients to innovate and connect your host country

Economies in the developed world are increasingly based on knowledge and innovation. The good news is that the UK is seen as innovative. The Ipsos Nation Brand Index in 2020 rated the UK in second place overall after Germany. The UK had been consistently placed near the top, hovering around third place in the previous five years since 2015. During the same period the United States had a fall from sixth to tenth place, reportedly due to a sharp fall in public opinion about its governance, trade tensions, immigration and investment. Fast forward to 2022 and the UK had dropped to sixth place, mostly due to falls in perception of its reputation and governance.

Back in my time at News Corp and EY, colleagues talked about building your personal brand. This is really important because nobody succeeds on their own. You need team mates, innovative collaborators, supporters, sponsors and customers. It works the same way for a country's reputation and brand. Talented people, nations and companies will want to work with stable, reputable and innovative countries. We need to regain Britain's reputation and prosperity.

A shared national purpose creates the focus needed to double our efforts exactly where it is critical to grow the British economy in ways that set us up for decades to come. We are not going to be able to compete on cost, so knowledge, innovation, and collaborating around the world to make sure the 'commercials' deliver for our country in my view is the way to unite.

We need to do this now, otherwise we are sleepwalking Britain into oblivion during our lifetime.

There are still many win-win scenarios if we are willing to create together and share the prosperity. The economy is not made up of a finite number of jobs, the economy can grow with more and better jobs with the diversity, problem solving and drive that come from migrant magic. I really enjoyed talking to Paula Bekinschtein, Senior Global Commercial and Operations Advisor at a biotech company:

> Both my husband and I are from Argentina. I studied Biotechnology back in Argentina and Genetics at the University of Cambridge. I have worked with multiple biopharma and healthcare organizations and projects in Cambridge and globally. It is really important to me to use my experience and network to contribute and mentor. I volunteer for multiple charities with the hope that I can offer to others what I wish I had when I first arrived in the UK.

 Migrants have all the attributes to become the special key to their host country's success and prosperity and they want nothing more than to be recognized.

One of the most driven, hard-working people I know, compelled to use her background to advocate and connect Britain, is Lin Yue, Executive Director at a leading global financial institution:

> For many Asian countries doing business is about relationships and trust. Having highly capable driven cheer leaders for British business is key in our competing globally, creating trade links. I came from China to the UK for my education. I am now a mother of two, working in a leading firm and am doing everything I can to promote collaboration.

One of the best ways to multiply the impact of your experience is by sharing your knowledge and story. For Ian Clarke, former Vice President, Global Banking Sales, at a large global banking institution, it all came together when he started his change consultancy business:

> Having spent 14 years in banking, I left to launch my own change consultancy in 2021. Founded on the principles by which I conduct myself and value most in others – real deeds, not words – my firm and I are committed to delivering meaningful positive change for those who need it most.

As humans we all need recognition and positive feedback. Beyond physical needs, we have the psychological need to be accepted in society as relevant, of value and belonging. Today's politics against migrants damages communities and economies but also takes away the dignity and confidence every human gets from being valued and accepted.

I understand how migrants may feel, but we need to together rise above this. Individually we need to dig deep and decide that no matter the negative messages, we know how valuable we are as migrants, and to then deliver on that value. We need to separate the politics from the people in our host country and to make contributions and care about the country we now belong to. Contribution is what gives you power and belonging. No matter how someone thinks of you or treats you, the choice to give away your power to them is yours.

Historically some governments and destructive leaders had a strategy to divide and conquer. Today there is a tendency to demonize marginalized groups and this is at times reflected in the media. This is regardless of specific political parties. People need to decide at some point that they are not going to be manipulated in this way and to unite behind the common causes of equality, equity and social mobility. As migrants we have a lot more in common with the

British people than you may realize. The way to unite is by contributing to each other's common causes and succeeding together.

Share the best parts of your culture and learn from your host

As I write this book, the 'culture wars' have been escalated by some, for a few votes and the attainment of power in politics or selling more media content which is increasingly difficult to monetize. Britain has arguably become more polarized than ever. This breaks my heart because my British friends have been so good to me at the most difficult times in my life. I still experience positive kindness every day, but also a brand of what I would call 'tribal prejudice' that I hadn't experienced for 30 years. I remember at one of the many schools I went to in the first few years in the UK, I made a few friends who were white British and a few who were Asian like me. There were some horrible moments where I was told by a couple of girls that I had to choose which group I belonged to. They told me that I couldn't be friends with both. I explained that I wanted to be friends with them all, but one or two did not accept that and I remember feeling very sad because I really liked them and we had plenty in common at a time that I needed it most. This was such an unnecessary loss for us all. I wasn't going to give in, though. Anyone who ever made their friendship conditional on excluding others, wasn't going to be my friend. Thirty years have passed and I have since found that people who are not inclusive in their decisions and behaviours do end up with an ever-shrinking circle.

This is what integration means to me; to learn the best parts of British culture and make friends, while not forgetting the best parts of our own culture and celebrating our heritage. If you manage to do this with balance in mind, there is no trade-off between integration and your cultural identity. This is not easy, I know, but the prize is your success as well as positive social impact on your host country and harmony in communities.

Talking to Akima Paul Lambert, Litigation Partner at a global law firm, reminded me about the cultural qualities we each bring. She really exemplifies a less individualistic culture, using her personal success for the greater good of her family:

> I think it is really important for migrants to think about wealth creation for their families. When I got my graduate job, I didn't live in Hampstead like my peers. I lived in a house share in Lewisham so I could send money back home. I couldn't get a mortgage to take

advantage of the housing market as I was on a visa. There are many barriers for migrants.

Migrants coming from countries with a greater need for industry and security transfer the best aspects of their culture and skills to the host country. We can all learn from each other and as a nation become stronger. It is human to want to share knowledge. Recognize the parts of your culture that lead to success.

Recognize and share the parts of your culture that lead to success and also be open to learning new ways from people in your host country. Think merit, not background.

If there is a large and established diaspora of people from your country of origin, do seek their help in settling into your host country. But do so without excluding the British, and make friends with and learn from all sorts of people. This leads to trust and positive regard between the host nation and migrants.

The big picture is in how we can together serve the common purpose. For me this is about growing the British economy and then making sure that prosperity generates opportunities for everyone regardless of their background. We will either all fail together or succeed together. This common purpose really motivates people to support you. This is intrinsic motivation which really sticks.

For us to succeed together we each need to make our individual contribution to that success. If there is one key takeaway I would like to give you, it is to use the lessons in this book to work out what direction you want to go in life and what components of knowledge, skills and transformational experiences you need to get there. It is about getting 'your energy sources' lined up working in the same direction to multiply your impact. If anything in your life is an energy working against your desired direction, distance yourself from it.

I am going to tell you one final story that shows you how different we each are and that part of your migrant magic is getting to know others and their individual motivations in order to also bring out the best in them.

When I was 16, my parents were divorcing and even though my father's strict rules still guided me in my mind, I had an opportunity I went for which I knew he would not be happy with. Up to that point, given my father's strictness, I had hardly talked to a boy unless he was my cousin. But one day my maths teacher's son turned up at our school for his mum. I saw him from a distance and realized who he was as he was talking to his mum. I thought he was good looking and really seemed like a good boy type which I really liked. Without hesitation I walked over to him and asked him out once my maths teacher had left. The poor boy looked shocked and after a short pause he managed to get a smile together and said ok. We met, I think it was in Cannon Hill Park, and he was lovely. But soon into the 'date' he mentioned how uncool maths was. Immediately I told him if he didn't like maths I couldn't go out with him and ended the date. I advised him to really think about improving his maths with more practice so that he would enjoy it as he got better at it. That of course was my first time ever being alone with a boy and effectively my first date.

Once I went to university and met other boys, I realized that wasn't typically what happens on a date. The next day at school my maths teacher had quite a grin on her face and I think she found what had happened amusing. Several years later when I was 23, I met my husband. On our first date I went to pick him up for dinner at my favourite Chinese restaurant, China Court, as I had a car. He asked me to come in when I arrived at his house. I hated being late for a booking but I agreed to go in. He looked quite excited and asked me to come upstairs. He took me into his bedroom and by now I was thinking he was up to no good and I was ready for a sharp exit. We entered his room and still smiling he turned on his computer, showed me his work and asked me if I liked his coding and wasn't his programme beautiful. People ask you if it was love at first sight and for me it was love at first sight of his coding. That was the moment I knew this is the guy for me. Not necessarily for the quality of his coding, which I am sure was excellent, but for the love and pride he showed towards his work.

To this day I can honestly say I have done things my way, and even with my father as a strong influence on me I have been one of the few people in his life who has comfortably said so when I disagreed with him.

Your mind, your path, your life. You only get one. You have to believe in your choices, and it is your belief that counts. Yes, you ask for advice from people you believe in and trust. You should also ask advice from people very different from you. But at the end, own your decisions.

I am at ease with my decisions, but there is one debate between me and my father which we haven't settled yet. The discussion is about nature versus nurture. He is much more in the nature camp and yet I believe our achievements come mostly from the lessons that our environment presents us with. He did recently say something. He said the environment is relevant but for centuries people had been routinely sitting under apple trees and yet it was only Newton who drew conclusions about gravity from the apple falling. I might have to let him win that one.

Acknowledgements

The path of gratitude is not for children; it is path of tender heroes, of the heroes of tenderness who, whatever happens, keep burning on the altar of their hearts the flame of adoration.
– Rumi

I am so grateful to countless individuals who have mentored, sponsored and supported me throughout my life. There are too many to mention them all here.

To my loving husband and children who are the meaning of my life. To my parents, grandparents, and my brother who I am so proud of. To everyone in my extended family who are truly my family. To the teachers who showed belief in me when I had lost belief in myself and the world. To the colleagues and friends who saw something in me when I possessed nothing. To the leaders who sponsored my endeavours. To the Migrant Leaders team, mentees, mentors and supporters who lift our charity and young people to greater heights every day. To Dr Yvonne Thompson CBE DL and Rene Carayol MBE for their belief and trust in me. To the Migrant Leaders mentors and supporters who endorsed the book and generously allowed their quotes to be mentioned in this book:

Ade Onagoruwa, Adrienne Larmond, Aimée Dushime, Akima Paul Lambert, Alejandra Alvarez Pineda, Alexandra Pluymackers, Alina Timofeeva, Alpesh Mistry, Ambily Banerjee, Asad Maqsood, Ashrina Parmar, Barbara Gottardi, Belen Solanas, Belgin Irmak, Bhavesh Mistry, Bilkis Shittu, Charlotte Harvey, Chris Williams, Cynthia V Davis CBE, Daniel Khan, Daniela Correia, Daniyaal Anawar, Divyesh Bilimoria, Dr Yvonne Thompson CBE DL, Dwayne Bonsu, Emily Southon, Emmanuel Nzolantima, Faiza A. Khan, Farid Froghi, Farley Thomas, Fationa Bejko, Frank Omare, Giovanni Sobrero, Harish Kumar, Hicham Daoud, Ian Clarke, Jamie Qiu, Javid Hamid, Joe Seddon, Kamelia Kantcheva, Katrina Borissova, Lee Chambers, Lin Yue, Mariama Nadworna, Mary Carmen Gasco-Buisson, Mona Bitar, Nehal Rajnikant Jilka, Nilofar Bhurawala, Nitin Parmar, Njideka Chima-Amaeshi, Parmesh Rajani, Paula Bekinschtein, Preetam Singh Heeramun, Professor Joanna Clarke, Professor Mary Bosworth, Purnima Sen, Rahul Welde, Rene Carayol MBE, Risham Nadeem, Ritika Wadhwa, Saeed Atcha MBE DL, Sami Ben-Ali, Sara Radenovic, Sayeh Ghanbari, Sunny Deo, Tanveer Kaur, Thomas John Sebastian, Trinh Tu, Wincie Wong.

About the author

Elham Fardad's defining moment came when at 18 she found herself penniless, with a separated family and many doors closed as a migrant coming from war-stricken Iran. She camped outside Birmingham city council offices for three days in a row until they agreed to count her as a home student so she could go to university.

Her first big career break came at the age of 25 when, as a newly qualified accountant, GE offered her a financial controller role in their GE Energy business. She spent the next few years as financial controller by day and Six Sigma rep by night, working with the business to integrate and transform the operational and commercial processes into a regional centre of excellence. She often describes that period as GE supporting her to fly, and during the same period, she completed her studies as the youngest Executive MBA from the University of Warwick.

Having created that early career momentum, Elham's lifelong dream came true when she got married and had her two children. During this time, she worked in various finance leadership roles at News Corp, turning around operational and financial performance across their businesses and immersing herself in motherhood.

Elham remembers how as a young teenager new to the UK, she would spend some Saturdays in Birmingham city centre going to the library, collecting free leaflets from banks, and selling perfumes door to door so she could buy fashionable clothes from Topshop. She describes how she discovered the EY office walking around in Colmore Row, looking up at the building and wondering if she could ever work in a place like that. Elham spent the next decade after News Corp at EY, working on some of the most challenging client problems. In her talks on gender parity and parenthood, she often mentions how EY's flexibility enabled her to use her hard-earned skills at work while prioritizing her children.

Having achieved her dreams, she eventually felt that she was leaving behind the people who would always be a part of her. She wanted to help the migrant families who make remarkable sacrifices in the hope that their children will succeed in their host countries; what Elham calls the 'Migrant Formula'. She launched the Migrant Leaders charity in 2017, and six years on, the charity has almost 2000 young mentees on its development programme of mentoring, workshops, work experiences and connections. In six years, she has met with over a thousand executives, recruiting them as mentors for the charity, and formed many corporate partnerships across FTSE100 and leading firms. Migrant Leaders was the winner of the Social Mobility Award 2023 at the prestigious Inclusive Awards. In 2023 Elham had the honour of being selected as a Coronation Champion.

Bibliography

'The Bigger Picture UK Social Mobility — A Tough Climb' (goldmansachs.com).

'Chart: The Top 10 Percent Own 70 Percent of U.S. Wealth', Statista.

'The Fiscal Effects of Immigration to the UK', UCL Department of Economics, University College London.

'The Fiscal Impact of Immigration on the UK' – Oxford Economics.

'Half of world's wealth now in hands of 1% of population' – report, Savings, *The Guardian*.

Ipsos Nation Brand Index 2020.

'Quarter of best-paid UK workers are migrants' (peoplemanagement.co.uk).

'Migrants in the UK: An Overview' – Migration Observatory (ox.ac.uk).

Ministry of Justice, 2019, 'Statistics on Race and the Criminal Justice System 2018'.

Lucinda Platt and Carolina V. Zuccotti, 2021, 'Social mobility and ethnicity', The Institute for Fiscal Studies Deaton Review.

Index